At Issue

The Ethics of
Medical Testing

Other Books in the At Issue Series:

Are Americans Overmedicated?

Are Newspapers Becoming Extinct?

Are Social Networking Sites Harmful?

Are Textbooks Biased?

Cell Phones and Driving

Food Safety

How Can the Poor Be Helped?

How Does Advertising Impact Teen Behavior?

Human Waste

Identity Theft

Media Bias

Pandemics

Rebuilding the World Trade Center Site

Should Religious Symbols Be Allowed on Public Land?

Should There Be An International Climate Treaty?

Student Loans

At Issue

The Ethics of
Medical Testing

Tamara Thompson, Book Editor

GREENHAVEN PRESS
A part of Gale, Cengage Learning

GALE
CENGAGE Learning·

Detroit • New York • San Francisco • New Haven, Conn • Waterville, Maine • London

Elizabeth Des Chenes, *Managing Editor*

For more information, contact:
Greenhaven Press
27500 Drake Rd.
Farmington Hills, MI 48331-3535
Or you can visit our Internet site at gale.cengage.com

For product information and technology assistance, contact us at

Gale Customer Support, 1-800-877-4253
For permission to use material from this text or product, submit all requests online at www.cengage.com/permissions

Further permissions questions can be e-mailed to permissionrequest@cengage.com.

Articles in Greenhaven Press anthologies are often edited for length to meet page requirements. In addition, original titles of these works are changed to clearly present the main thesis and to explicitly indicate the author's opinion. Every effort is made to ensure that Greenhaven Press accurately reflects the original intent of the authors. Every effort has been made to trace the owners of copyrighted material.

Cover Image copyright © Images.com/Corbis.

LIBRARY OF CONGRESS CATALOGING-IN-PUBLICATION DATA

The ethics of medical testing / Tamara Thompson, editor.
    p. cm. -- (At issue)
    Includes bibliographical references and index.
    ISBN 978-0-7377-5902-0 (hardback) -- ISBN 978-0-7377-5903-7 (paperback)
    1. Medicine--Research--Moral and ethical aspects--Juvenile literature. I. Thompson, Tamara. II. Title. III. Series.
    R724.E247 2011
    174.2'8--dc23
                                      2011028550

Printed in the United States of America
1 2 3 4 5 6 7 15 14 13 12 11

Contents

Introduction   7

1. Modern Medical Testing Is Shaped   12
   by a Troubled Legacy
   Associated Press

2. Strict Guidelines Ensure Safe and Ethical   22
   Medical Testing on Humans
   Pharmaceutical Research and Manufacturers
   of America

3. Medical Testing on Humans Can Be   33
   Dangerous and Corrupt
   Paul Tosto and Jeremy Olson

4. Review Boards Are Inadequate to Ensure   39
   Ethical Medical Testing
   Mary Beckman

5. Medical Testing on Prisoners Is Unethical   45
   and Should Be Outlawed
   Silja J.A. Talvi

6. Medical Testing on Prisoners Can   51
   Be Done Ethically
   Institute of Medicine

7. Medical Testing on Children Involves Unique   58
   Ethical Considerations
   Donna Sylvester and Tonia Morrison

8. Special Rules Can Provide Safeguards   64
   for Vulnerable Test Populations
   David Wendler and Christine Grady

9. Using Animals for Medical Testing   76
   Is Unethical and Unnecessary
   People for the Ethical Treatment of Animals
   (PETA)

10. Using Animals for Medical Testing   83
    Is Both Ethical and Essential
    Foundation for Biomedical Research

11. Genetic Testing Necessitates New   92
    Ethical Considerations
    *North Carolina Association
    for Biomedical Research*

12. Medical Testing in Developing Countries   104
    Is Conducted Ethically
    Todd D. Clark

13. Ethicists Disagree About Medical Testing   110
    Without Consent During Crises
    Rob Stein

Organizations to Contact   116

Bibliography   121

Index   126

Introduction

The high standard of modern medical care available today owes a great debt to the testing of procedures, devices, and medicines on human research subjects. But while the benefit to humanity is undeniable, it often has come at a steep price. Although medical testing of various forms is now heavily regulated in the United States, it has a dark and disturbing history that is filled with ethically corrupt and cruel practices whose legacies cast a long shadow into the present.

While many people know that Nazi doctors conducted unspeakable medical experiments on concentration camp prisoners during World War II, few realize that grotesque and unethical medical testing also took place in the United States—often without consent—well into the 1970s. The accounts read like some kind of twisted plotline from a medical thriller. Physicians repeatedly conducted vivisections (non-necessary experimental surgeries) on women without anesthesia to develop an understanding of gynecology. Researchers deliberately infected thousands of people with deadly diseases such as syphilis, tuberculosis, bubonic plague, cholera, malaria, and cancer without their knowledge, often withholding treatment so they could study the progress of the diseases; they conducted spinal taps and electroshock therapy on toddlers, just to see what would happen; they infected developmentally disabled children with viral hepatitis by feeding them infected feces (but telling the parents it was a vaccine); they surgically implanted the testicles of dead humans and animals into able-bodied, healthy men; they injected people with toxic and radioactive chemicals and inserted radium rods into the noses of schoolchildren to learn about the effects of Cold War technologies; they applied skin-blistering substances to the faces and backs of prisoners to see how badly they would be disfigured; they subjected pregnant women to drugs that caused birth defects and miscarriages; and they infected hundreds of mental patients with sexually transmitted diseases.

More often than not, the participants in such medical experimentation were members of marginalized groups, such as the mentally disabled, the poor, the illiterate, racial minorities, or prisoners. Researchers at the time defended their experiments on these groups as ethically acceptable because of the benefit they brought to science. But as Sonia Shah writes in her book *The Body Hunters*, "Nazi medical experimentation may have fallen into a lower category of depravity than what was happening in the United States, conducted as it was in the context of wholesale butchery, but the fact was that little could be called upon to prove this was so, at least not without knocking the medical profession off its pedestal." And indeed, that is just what ultimately had to happen for human research subjects to receive legal protection.

The Nuremberg Code, set forth after World War II in response to war-time medical atrocities, was the first document to articulate a code of research ethics and protections for human research participants. It established ten ethical guidelines for research—including the enduring tenets of voluntary and informed consent, the right to opt out of participation, and the idea that the risk to a participant from a study should not outweigh the humanitarian benefit. Building on that, in 1964, the World Medical Association drafted the Declaration of Helsinki, which was signed by thirty-four countries, including the United States. The declaration remains the cornerstone of research ethics for much of the world, and it laid the groundwork for the institutional review board (IRB) process that is a standard component of medical research today. An IRB is a committee that approves, monitors, and reviews studies and experiments involving humans and protects the rights and well-being of participants.

The Nuremberg and Helsinki documents are both voluntary, however, not legally binding, and it was not until 1974 that the United States adopted any legal protections of its own for human research participants. The move came in response to public outrage over a newspaper investigation of the Tuskegee Syphilis Experiment, a clinical study conducted between 1932 and 1972 in Tuskegee, Alabama, by the US Public Health Service. In the study, four hundred impoverished black men who had syphilis were told they were being treated for the deadly disease, but the researchers secretly gave them nothing, even though penicillin was known to cure their ailment. The researchers simply observed the effects of syphilis on the men's bodies, and by the end of the study only seventy-four of the test subjects were still alive. Additionally, forty of their wives were infected, and nineteen children were born with the disease.

Cited by Ralph V. Katz and colleagues in a November 2006 *Journal of Health Care for the Poor and Underserved* article on the Tuskeegee Legacy Project as "arguably the most infamous biomedical research study in U.S. history," the Tuskegee study prompted a congressional investigation, followed by the publication of the pivotal Belmont Report. The report led to the establishment of the federal Office for Human Research Protections (OHRP) and became the basis for modern federal regulations and the establishment of IRBs for the protection of human research subjects.

Nearly two decades after the study, on May 16, 1997, President Bill Clinton formally apologized to the eight remaining Tuskegee survivors: "What was done cannot be undone," said Clinton, "but we can end the silence. We can stop turning our heads away. We can look at you in the eye and finally say on behalf of the American people, what the United States government did was shameful, and I am sorry."

In the years since Tuskegee, the rights and safety of study participants and the moral and ethical responsibilities of researchers have been brought into sharp focus, but at the same time the legal restrictions and increased scrutiny have meant rising costs and time delays for researchers. In response, instead of conducting clinical trials of new drugs in the United States, pharmaceutical companies increasingly are exporting their studies to developing countries where it is cheaper and less restrictive to conduct research on humans. According to the University of Hong Kong Clinical Trials Centre, a quarter of all global drug trials are now being conducted in developing countries such as India, Estonia, and Nigeria. From 1988 to 2008, the number grew by 2,000 percent, to approximately sixty-five hundred trials.

Critics argue there is little accountability for foreign trials and—like in the early days of medical testing in the United States—they often are conducted with poor and illiterate people who may feel financially pressured to participate and who may not understand the consequences of their participation. US authorities rarely monitor foreign trials, they claim, and the standards of acceptable care differ greatly from what is expected in the United States. As Shah notes, "If the history of human experimentation tells us anything, from the bloody vivisections of the first millennium to the Tuskegee Syphilis Study, it is that the potential for abuse will fall heaviest on the poor and most powerless among us."

The American pharmaceutical industry, however, defends its research practices and maintains that it does a good job of policing itself on ethical matters. "Is it ethical to conduct such studies outside of the United States? In a word: Yes," says Ken Johnson, senior vice president of Pharmaceutical Research and Manufacturers of America (PhRMA), an organization that represents US drug research and biotechnology companies. In his June 27, 2010, statement on behalf of PhRMA, Johnson continued, declaring, "The same strict regulatory standards apply to foreign trials as trials conducted domestically." Industry leaders also note that research participants in poor countries get an extra benefit because they receive therapies through the studies that would otherwise be unavailable to them.

Whether the future of medical testing will be a bright contribution to global health, as the industry purports, or whether it heralds a backsliding to the unethical practices of the past, as critics warn, remains to be seen. The authors of the viewpoints in *At Issue: The Ethics of Medical Testing* present a wide range of concerns over the benefits and consequences of medical testing in the past, present, and future.

1

Modern Medical Testing Is Shaped by a Troubled Legacy

Associated Press

The Associated Press is a wire service.

Medical testing has a grim history of serious ethical lapses that continue to have lingering effects. In the early days of human experimentation, it was deemed acceptable to experiment on people without their consent and even to deliberately give them terrible diseases and then study their progress rather than to cure them. Painful and unnecessary procedures often were carried out more in the name of curiosity than of medical advancement. The publicizing of three highly unethical studies in the 1970s helped turn public opinion against such practices and led to government reforms. But rather than be bound by the new guidelines, many researchers began conducting experiments and clinical trials in countries that do not have such laws, a trend that continues today. President Barack Obama's presidential bioethics commission must confront the ethics of foreign trials even as past abuses are still coming to light.

Shocking as it may seem, U.S. government doctors once thought it was fine to experiment on disabled people and prison inmates. Such experiments included giving hepatitis to mental patients in Connecticut, squirting a pandemic flu virus up the noses of prisoners in Maryland, and injecting cancer cells into chronically ill people at a New York hospital.

Much of this horrific history is 40 to 80 years old, but it is the backdrop for a meeting in Washington this week [February 2011] by a presidential bioethics commission. The meeting was triggered by the government's apology last fall [2010] for federal doctors infecting prisoners and mental patients in Guatemala with syphilis 65 years ago.

U.S. officials also acknowledged there had been dozens of similar experiments in the United States—studies that often involved making healthy people sick.

An exhaustive review by The Associated Press of medical journal reports and decades-old press clippings found more than 40 such studies. At best, these were a search for lifesaving treatments; at worst, some amounted to curiosity-satisfying experiments that hurt people but provided no useful results.

Inevitably, they will be compared to the well-known Tuskegee syphilis study. In that episode, U.S. health officials tracked 600 black men in Alabama who already had syphilis but didn't give them adequate treatment even after penicillin became available.

Many prominent researchers felt it was legitimate to experiment on people who did not have full rights in society—people like prisoners, mental patients, poor blacks.

Participants Deliberately Given Diseases

These studies were worse in at least one respect—they violated the concept of "first do no harm," a fundamental medical principle that stretches back centuries.

"When you give somebody a disease—even by the standards of their time—you really cross the key ethical norm of the profession," said Arthur Caplan, director of the University of Pennsylvania's Center for Bioethics.

Some of these studies, mostly from the 1940s to the '60s, apparently were never covered by news media. Others were reported at the time, but the focus was on the promise of enduring new cures, while glossing over how test subjects were treated.

Attitudes about medical research were different then. Infectious diseases killed many more people years ago, and doctors worked urgently to invent and test cures. Many prominent researchers felt it was legitimate to experiment on people who did not have full rights in society—people like prisoners, mental patients, poor blacks. It was an attitude in some ways similar to that of Nazi doctors experimenting on Jews.

"There was definitely a sense—that we don't have today—that sacrifice for the nation was important," said Laura Stark, a Wesleyan University assistant professor of science in society, who is writing a book about past federal medical experiments.

Review of Past Research

- A federally funded study begun in 1942 injected experimental flu vaccine in male patients at a state insane asylum in Ypsilanti, Mich., then exposed them to flu several months later. It was co-authored by Dr. Jonas Salk, who a decade later would become famous as inventor of the polio vaccine.

  Some of the men weren't able to describe their symptoms, raising serious questions about how well they understood what was being done to them. One newspaper account mentioned the test subjects were "senile and debilitated." Then it quickly moved on to the promising results.

- In federally funded studies in the 1940s, noted researcher Dr. W. Paul Havens Jr. exposed men to hepatitis in a series of experiments, including one using patients from mental institutions in Middletown and Norwich, Conn. Havens, a World Health Organization expert on viral diseases, was one of the first scientists to differentiate types of hepatitis and their causes.

A search of various news archives found no mention of the mental patients study, which made eight healthy men ill but broke no new ground in understanding the disease.

- Researchers in the mid-1940s studied the transmission of a deadly stomach bug by having young men swallow unfiltered stool suspension. The study was conducted at the New York State Vocational Institution, a reformatory prison in West Coxsackie. The point was to see how well the disease spread that way as compared to spraying the germs and having test subjects breathe it. Swallowing it was a more effective way to spread the disease, the researchers concluded. The study doesn't explain if the men were rewarded for this awful task.

- A University of Minnesota study in the late 1940s injected 11 public service employee volunteers with malaria, then starved them for five days. Some were also subjected to hard labor, and those men lost an average of 14 pounds. They were treated for malarial fevers with quinine sulfate. One of the authors was Ancel Keys, a noted dietary scientist who developed K-rations for the military and the Mediterranean diet for the public. But a search of various news archives found no mention of the study.

- For a study in 1957, when the Asian flu pandemic was spreading, federal researchers sprayed the virus in the noses of 23 inmates at Patuxent prison in Jessup, Md., to compare their reactions to those of 32 virus-exposed inmates who had been given a new vaccine.

- Government researchers in the 1950s tried to infect about two dozen volunteering prison inmates with gonorrhea using two different methods in an experiment at a federal penitentiary in Atlanta. The bacteria was pumped directly into the urinary tract through the penis, according to their paper.

> The men quickly developed the disease, but the researchers noted this method wasn't comparable to how men normally got infected—by having sex with an infected partner. The men were later treated with antibiotics. The study was published in the *Journal of the American Medical Association*, but there was no mention of it in various news archives.

Though people in the studies were usually described as volunteers, historians and ethicists have questioned how well these people understood what was to be done to them and why, or whether they were coerced.

Prisoners have long been victimized for the sake of science.

Studies Involving Prisoners

Prisoners have long been victimized for the sake of science. In 1915, the U.S. government's Dr. Joseph Goldberger—today remembered as a public health hero—recruited Mississippi inmates to go on special rations to prove his theory that the painful illness pellagra was caused by a dietary deficiency. (The men were offered pardons for their participation.)

But studies using prisoners were uncommon in the first few decades of the 20th century, and usually performed by researchers considered eccentric even by the standards of the day. One was Dr. L.L. Stanley, resident physician at San Quentin prison in California, who around 1920 attempted to treat older, "devitalized men" by implanting in them testicles from livestock and from recently executed convicts.

Newspapers wrote about Stanley's experiments, but the lack of outrage is striking.

"Enter San Quentin penitentiary in the role of the Fountain of Youth—an institution where the years are made to roll back for men of failing mentality and vitality and where the spring is restored to the step, wit to the brain, vigor to the muscles and ambition to the spirit. All this has been done, is being done . . . by a surgeon with a scalpel," began one rosy report published in November 1919 in *The Washington Post*.

Around the time of World War II, prisoners were enlisted to help the war effort by taking part in studies that could help the troops. For example, a series of malaria studies at Stateville Penitentiary in Illinois and two other prisons was designed to test antimalarial drugs that could help soldiers fighting in the Pacific.

It was at about this time that prosecution of Nazi doctors in 1947 led to the "Nuremberg Code," a set of international rules to protect human test subjects. Many U.S. doctors essentially ignored them, arguing that they applied to Nazi atrocities—not to American medicine.

The late 1940s and 1950s saw huge growth in the U.S. pharmaceutical and health care industries, accompanied by a boom in prisoner experiments funded by both the government and corporations. By the 1960s, at least half the states allowed prisoners to be used as medical guinea pigs.

But two studies in the 1960s proved to be turning points in the public's attitude toward the way test subjects were treated.

The first came to light in 1963. Researchers injected cancer cells into 19 old and debilitated patients at a Jewish Chronic Disease Hospital in the New York borough of Brooklyn to see if their bodies would reject them.

The hospital director said the patients were not told they were being injected with cancer cells because there was no need—the cells were deemed harmless. But the experiment upset a lawyer named William Hyman who sat on the hospital's board of directors. The state investigated, and the hospital ultimately said any such experiments would require the patient's written consent.

The Eventual Backlash

At nearby Staten Island, from 1963 to 1966, a controversial medical study was conducted at the Willowbrook State School for children with mental retardation. The children were intentionally given hepatitis orally and by injection to see if they could then be cured with gamma globulin.

Those two studies—along with the Tuskegee experiment revealed in 1972—proved to be a "holy trinity" that sparked extensive and critical media coverage and public disgust, said Susan Reverby, the Wellesley College historian who first discovered records of the syphilis study in Guatemala.

By the early 1970s, even experiments involving prisoners were considered scandalous. In widely covered congressional hearings in 1973, pharmaceutical industry officials acknowledged they were using prisoners for testing because they were cheaper than chimpanzees.

Holmesburg Prison in Philadelphia made extensive use of inmates for medical experiments. Some of the victims are still around to talk about it. Edward "Yusef" Anthony, featured in a book about the studies, says he agreed to have a layer of skin peeled off his back, which was coated with searing chemicals to test a drug. He did that for money to buy cigarettes in prison.

"I said 'Oh my God, my back is on fire! Take this . . . off me!'" Anthony said in an interview with The Associated Press, as he recalled the beginning of weeks of intense itching and agonizing pain.

The government responded with reforms. Among them: The U.S. Bureau of Prisons in the mid-1970s effectively excluded all research by drug companies and other outside agencies within federal prisons.

As the supply of prisoners and mental patients dried up, researchers looked to other countries.

It made sense. Clinical trials could be done more cheaply and with fewer rules. And it was easy to find patients who were taking no medication, a factor that can complicate tests of other drugs.

Additional sets of ethical guidelines have been enacted, and few believe that another Guatemala study could happen today. "It's not that we're out infecting anybody with things," Caplan said.

Between 40 and 65 percent of clinical studies of federally regulated medical products were done in other countries in 2008.

Modern Studies Unethical, Too

Still, in the last 15 years, two international studies sparked outrage.

One was likened to Tuskegee. U.S.-funded doctors failed to give the AIDS drug AZT to all the HIV-infected pregnant women in a study in Uganda even though it would have protected their newborns. U.S. health officials argued the study would answer questions about AZT's use in the developing world.

The other study, by Pfizer Inc., gave an antibiotic named Trovan to children with meningitis in Nigeria, although there were doubts about its effectiveness for that disease. Critics blamed the experiment for the deaths of 11 children and the disabling of scores of others. Pfizer settled a lawsuit with Nigerian officials for $75 million but admitted no wrongdoing.

Last year [2010], the U.S. Department of Health and Human Services' inspector general reported that between 40 and 65 percent of clinical studies of federally regulated medical products were done in other countries in 2008, and that proportion probably has grown. The report also noted that U.S. regulators inspected fewer than 1 percent of foreign clinical trial sites.

Monitoring research is complicated, and rules that are too rigid could slow new drug development. But it's often hard to get information on international trials, sometimes because of missing records and a paucity [scarcity] of audits, said Dr. Kevin Schulman, a Duke University professor of medicine who has written on the ethics of international studies.

It was clear that people in the study did not understand what was being done to them or were not able to give their consent.

These issues were still being debated when, last October [2010], the Guatemala study came to light.

In the 1946–48 study, American scientists infected prisoners and patients in a mental hospital in Guatemala with syphilis, apparently to test whether penicillin could prevent some sexually transmitted disease. The study came up with no useful information and was hidden for decades.

The Guatemala study nauseated ethicists on multiple levels. Beyond infecting patients with a terrible illness, it was clear that people in the study did not understand what was being done to them or were not able to give their consent. Indeed, though it happened at a time when scientists were quick to publish research that showed frank disinterest in the rights of study participants, this study was buried in file drawers.

"It was unusually unethical, even at the time," said Stark, the Wesleyan researcher.

Could It Happen Today?

"When the president was briefed on the details of the Guatemalan episode, one of his first questions was whether this sort of thing could still happen today," said Rick Weiss, a spokesman for the White House Office of Science and Technology Policy.

That it occurred overseas was an opening for the [Barack] Obama administration to have the bioethics panel seek a new evaluation of international medical studies. The president also asked the Institute of Medicine [IOM] to further probe the Guatemala study, but the IOM relinquished the assignment in November [2010], after reporting its own conflict of interest: In the 1940s, five members of one of the IOM's sister organizations played prominent roles in federal syphilis research and had links to the Guatemala study.

So the bioethics commission gets both tasks. To focus on federally funded international studies, the commission has formed an international panel of about a dozen experts in ethics, science and clinical research. Regarding the look at the Guatemala study, the commission has hired 15 staff investigators and is working with additional historians and other consulting experts.

The panel is to send a report to Obama by September [2011]. Any further steps would be up to the administration.

Some experts say that given such a tight deadline, it would be a surprise if the commission produced substantive new information about past studies. "They face a really tough challenge," Caplan said.

2

Strict Guidelines Ensure Safe and Ethical Medical Testing on Humans

Pharmaceutical Research and Manufacturers of America

The Pharmaceutical Research and Manufacturers of America (PhRMA) is a lobbying organization that represents the country's leading pharmaceutical research and biotechnology companies.

Medical testing on human subjects provides many benefits to society, and even to some study participants, but also involves risks. Comprehensive guidelines ensure that such research is conducted ethically and that participants are protected. Researchers are required to adhere to the highest ethical standards concerning acquiring informed consent from study participants; potential conflicts of interest for researchers; the physical and emotional well-being of study participants; the specifics of the study design itself; the makeup of institutional review boards; safety and trial monitoring; payments to participants; privacy and confidentiality; and the reporting of data, among other things. Medical researchers recognize the importance of adhering to such standards because without a strong ethical framework study results would not be reliable or respected.

The Pharmaceutical Research and Manufacturers of America (PhRMA) represents research-based pharmaceutical and biotechnology companies. Our members discover, develop, manufacture and market new medicines and vaccines to enable patients to live longer and healthier lives.

Pharmaceutical Research and Manufacturers of America, *Principles on Conduct of Clinical Trials and Communication of Clinical Trial Results*. Washington, DC: PhRMA, 2009, pp. 1–20. Reproduced by permission.

The development of new therapies to treat disease and improve quality of life is a long and complex process. A critical part of that process is clinical research, the study of a pharmaceutical product in humans (research participants). Clinical research involves both potential benefits and risks to the participants and to society at large. Investigational clinical research is conducted to answer specific questions, and some aspects of the therapeutic profile (benefits and risks) of the product(s) tested cannot be fully known without study in humans. In sponsoring and conducting clinical research, PhRMA members place great importance on respecting and protecting the safety of research participants.

Principles for the conduct of clinical research are set forth in internationally recognized documents, such as the Declaration of Helsinki and the Guideline for Good Clinical Practice of the International Conference on Harmonization (ICH). The principles of these and similar reference standards are translated into legal requirements through laws and regulations enforced by national authorities such as the U.S. Food and Drug Administration (FDA). PhRMA members have always been committed, and remain committed, to sponsoring clinical research that fully complies with all legal and regulatory requirements.

A Collaborative Effort

Many different entities and individuals contribute to the safe and appropriate conduct of clinical research, including not only sponsoring companies but also regulatory agencies; investigative site staff and medical professionals who serve as clinical investigators; hospitals and other institutions where research is conducted; and institutional review boards and ethics committees (IRBs/ECs).

PhRMA adopts these voluntary Principles to clarify our members' relationships with other individuals and entities involved in the clinical research process and to set forth the principles we follow.

The key issues addressed here are:

• Protecting Research Participants

• Conduct of Clinical Trials

• Ensuring Objectivity in Research

• Providing Information About Clinical Trials

These Principles reinforce our commitment to the safety of research participants, and they provide guidance to address issues that bear on this commitment in the context of clinical trials that enroll research participants and are designed, conducted and sponsored by member companies.

For purposes of these Principles, a "clinical trial" means an interventional trial involving human subjects from Phase 1 and beyond. For example, the term does not include the use of a drug in the normal course of medical practice or non-clinical laboratory studies.

These revised Principles [took] effect on October 1, 2009.

Scientific, ethical and clinical judgments must guide and support the design of the clinical trial, particularly those aspects directly affecting the research participants.

How Trials Work

We conduct clinical research in a manner that recognizes the importance of protecting the safety of and respecting research participants. Our interactions with research participants, as well as with clinical investigators and the other persons and entities involved in clinical research, recognize this fundamental principle and reinforce the precautions established to protect research participants.

We conduct high quality clinical research, including trials and observational studies, to test scientific hypotheses rigorously and gather bona fide scientific data in accordance with applicable laws and regulations, as well as locally recognized good clinical practice, wherever in the world clinical trials are undertaken. When conducting multinational, multi-site trials, in both the industrialized and developing world, we follow standards based on the Guideline for Good Clinical Practice of the ICH. In addition, clinical trial protocols are reviewed by independent IRBs/ECs as well as national health authorities.

Clinical Trial Design. Sponsors conduct clinical trials based on scientifically designed protocols, which balance potential risk to the research participant with the possible benefit to the participant and to society. Scientific, ethical and clinical judgments must guide and support the design of the clinical trial, particularly those aspects directly affecting the research participants such as inclusion/exclusion criteria, endpoints, and choice of control, including active and/or placebo comparator.

Selection of Investigators. Investigators are selected based on qualifications, training, research or clinical expertise in relevant fields, the potential to recruit research participants and the ability to conduct clinical trials in accordance with good clinical practices and applicable legal requirements.

Training of Investigators. Investigators and their staff are trained on the clinical trial protocol, pharmaceutical product, and procedural issues associated with the conduct of the particular clinical trial.

We require that clinical investigators obtain and document informed consent, freely given without coercion, from all potential research participants.

IRB/EC Review. Prior to commencement, each clinical trial protocol is reviewed by an IRB/EC that has independent decision-making authority, and has the responsibility and authority to protect research participants.

- The IRB/EC has the right to disapprove, require changes, or approve the clinical trial before any participants are enrolled at the institution or investigative site for which it has responsibility.

- The IRB/EC is provided relevant information from prior studies, the clinical trial protocol, and any materials developed to inform potential participants about the proposed research.

Informed Consent. We require that clinical investigators obtain and document informed consent, freely given without coercion, from all potential research participants.

- Potential research participants are to be adequately informed about potential benefits and risks, alternative procedures or treatments, nature and duration of the clinical trial, and provided the opportunity to ask questions about the study and receive answers from a qualified healthcare professional associated with the trial.

- Clinical investigators should disclose to potential research participants during the informed consent process that the investigator and/or the institution is receiving payment for the conduct of the clinical trial.

- In those cases where research participants—for reasons such as age, illness, or injury—are incapable of giving their consent, the informed consent of a legally acceptable representative is required.

- Because participation in a clinical trial is voluntary, all research participants have the right to withdraw from continued participation in the clinical trial, at any time, without penalty or loss of benefits to which they are otherwise entitled.

Clinical Trial Monitoring. Trials are monitored using appropriately trained and qualified individuals. The sponsor will have procedures for these individuals to report on the progress of the trial, including possible scientific misconduct.

- These individuals verify compliance with good clinical practices, including (but not limited to) adherence to the clinical trial protocol, enrollment of appropriate research participants, and the accuracy and complete reporting of clinical trial data.

- If a sponsor learns that a clinical investigator is significantly deficient in any area, it will either work with the investigator to obtain compliance or discontinue the investigator's participation in the study, and notify the relevant authorities as required.

Ongoing Safety Monitoring. All safety issues are tracked and monitored in order to understand the safety profile of the product under study. Significant new safety information will be shared promptly with the clinical investigators and any Data and Safety Monitoring Board or Committee (DSMB), and reported to regulatory authorities in accordance with applicable law.

Privacy and Confidentiality of Medical Information. Sponsors respect the privacy rights of research participants and safeguard the confidentiality of their medical information in accordance with all applicable laws and regulations.

Quality Assurance. Procedures are followed to ensure that trials are conducted in accordance with good clinical practices and that data are generated, documented and reported accurately and in compliance with all applicable requirements.

Clinical Trials Conducted in the Developing World. When conducting clinical trials in the developing world, sponsors collaborate with investigators and seek to collaborate with other relevant parties, such as local health authorities and host governments, to address issues associated with the conduct of the proposed study and its follow-up.

Objectivity in Research

We respect the independence of the individuals and entities involved in the clinical research process, so that they can exercise their judgment for the purpose of protecting research participants and to ensure an objective and balanced interpretation of trial results. Our contracts and interactions with them will not interfere with this independence.

Independent Review and Safety Monitoring. In certain studies, generally large, randomized, multi-site studies that evaluate interventions intended to prolong life or reduce risk of a major adverse health outcome, the patients, investigators and the sponsor may each be blinded to the treatment each participant receives to avoid the introduction of bias into the study. In such cases, monitoring of interim study results and of new information from external sources by a DSMB may be appropriate to protect the welfare of the research participants. If a DSMB is established, its members should have varied expertise, including relevant fields of medicine, statistics, and bioethics. Sponsors help establish, and also respect, the independence of DSMBs.

- Clinical investigators participating in a clinical trial of a pharmaceutical product should not serve on a DSMB that is monitoring that trial. It is also not appropriate for such an investigator to serve on DSMBs monitoring other trials with the same product if knowledge accessed through the DSMB membership may influence his or her objectivity.

- A voting member of a DSMB should not have significant financial interests or other conflicts of interest that would preclude objective determinations. Employees of the sponsor may not serve as members of the DSMB, but may otherwise assist the DSMB in its evaluation of clinical trial data.

Payment to Research Participants. Research participants provide a valuable service to society. They take time out of their daily lives and sometimes incur expenses associated with their participation in clinical trials. When payments are made to research participants:

- Any proposed payment should be reviewed and approved by an independent IRB/EC.

- Payments should be based on research participants' time and/or reimbursement for reasonable expenses incurred during their participation in a clinical trial, such as parking, travel, and lodging expenses. Payment may be monetary and/or consist of items of modest value based on the factors noted above.

- The nature and amount of compensation or any other benefit should be consistent with the principle of voluntary informed consent.

Payment to Clinical Investigators. Payment to clinical investigators or their institutions should be reasonable and based on work performed by the investigator and the investigator's staff, not on any other considerations.

- A written contract or budgetary agreement should be in place, specifying the nature of the research services to be provided and the basis for payment for those services.

- Payments or compensation of any sort should not be tied to the outcome of clinical trials.

- Clinical investigators or their immediate family should not have a direct ownership interest in the specific pharmaceutical product being studied.

- Clinical investigators and institutions should not be compensated in company stock or stock options for work performed on individual clinical trials.

- When enrollment is particularly challenging, reasonable additional payments may be made to compensate the clinical investigator or institution for time and effort spent on extra recruiting efforts to enroll appropriate research participants.

- When clinical investigators and their staff are required to travel to meetings in conjunction with a clinical trial, they may be compensated for their time and offered reimbursement for reasonable travel, lodging, and meal expenses. The venue and circumstances should be appropriate for the purpose of the meeting; specifically, resorts are not appropriate venues. While modest meals or receptions may be appropriate during company-sponsored meetings with investigators, companies should not provide recreational or entertainment events in conjunction with these meetings. It is not appropriate to pay honoraria or travel or lodging expenses for those who are not involved in the clinical trial.

A potential conflict of interest exists in the research setting whenever an investigator's professional judgment could be influenced by a secondary interest.

Potential Conflicts of Interest

A potential conflict of interest exists, in the research setting, whenever an investigator's professional judgment could be influenced by a secondary interest, such as a potential financial gain, career advancement, outside employment, personal considerations or relationships, investments, gifts, payment for services, and board memberships. In the strict sense, some conflict of interest may exist in all research settings. For example, physicians who are specialists and/or leaders in their field are often extensively engaged by both the private and public sectors to provide their expertise. Further, by the nature of their practices, there are often a limited number of physicians who are best qualified to ensure that a specific trial will be able to reach and enroll the required number of patients. Physicians are subject to an array of professional standards and ethical obligations, including institutional disclosure policies and government regulations regarding disclosure of potential financial conflicts of interest in clinical research during the drug approval process. Companies should recognize and support physicians and researchers in meeting these standards and ethical obligations, including the following requirements for authorship:

- When authors submit a manuscript to a medical journal, whether an article or a letter, they are responsible for disclosing all financial and personal relationships that might bias their work. To prevent ambiguity, authors should state explicitly whether potential conflicts do or do not exist.

- Authors should identify individuals who provide writing or other assistance and disclose the funding source for this assistance. Authors should describe the role of the study sponsor(s), if any, in study design; in the collection, analysis, and interpretation of data; in the writing of the report; and in the decision to submit the report for publication. If the sponsor had no such involvement, the authors should so state.

We design and conduct clinical trials in an ethical and scientifically rigorous manner to determine the benefits, risks, and value of pharmaceutical products.

Providing Information

America's pharmaceutical research companies are committed to the transparency of clinical trials that are sponsored by our member companies. We recognize that there are important public health benefits associated with making appropriate clinical trial information widely available to healthcare practitioners, patients, and others. Such disclosure must maintain protections for individual privacy, intellectual property, and contract rights, as well as conform to legislation and current national practices in patent law.

Availability of information about clinical trials and their results in a timely manner is often critical to communicate important new information to the medical profession, patients and the public. We design and conduct clinical trials in an ethical and scientifically rigorous manner to determine the benefits, risks, and value of pharmaceutical products. As sponsors, we are responsible for receipt and verification of data from all research sites for the studies we conduct; we ensure the accuracy and integrity of the entire study database, which is owned by the sponsor.

Clinical trials may involve already marketed products and/or investigational products. We commit to the timely submission and registration on a public database of summary information about all clinical trials that we conduct involving the use of our marketed or investigational products in patients. We also commit to the timely submission and posting of summary results of all clinical trials conducted in patients involving the use of our products that are approved for marketing, or that are investigational products whose development programs are discontinued, regardless of outcome. In addition, if information from any clinical trial is felt to be of significant medical importance, then we will work with investigators to publish the data.

3

Medical Testing on Humans Can Be Dangerous and Corrupt

Paul Tosto and Jeremy Olson

Paul Tosto and Jeremy Olson are staff writers at the St. Paul Pioneer Press, *a Minnesota daily newspaper.*

Although regulations and institutional review boards (IRBs) are supposed to ensure that medical testing is conducted ethically and safely, they are not always enough. One example is the case of Dan Markingson, a schizophrenic who killed himself while participating in a clinical trial of antipsychotic drugs. The trial design specified that Markingson receive only one experimental medication rather than the several proven ones he would have otherwise been given for his condition. Critics say that withholding such standard care is unethical and that the problem was compounded by the fact that no one involved with the study took Markingson's family's concerns about his deteriorating condition seriously. The study was not halted after his death, as it should have been, and there was also a serious conflict of interest because the lead researcher was also Markingson's psychiatrist. No government agency tracks deaths or injuries caused by medical testing, and some health care experts believe that the nation's system of clinical trial oversight is badly in need of overhaul.

When people enter drug studies at the University of Minnesota [the U], they're supposed to be protected by a safety net keeping watch that the vulnerable are not coerced,

Paul Tosto and Jeremy Olson, "Patient's Suicide Raises Questions," *Pioneer Press*, May 23, 2008. Reproduced by permission.

that standards of conduct are met and that researchers aren't tangled in conflicts that might influence their decision-making.

That system was supposed to protect Dan Markingson.

A schizophrenic, Markingson killed himself in 2004 while enrolled in a study at the U comparing anti-psychotic drugs. Documents surfacing the past year in a lawsuit over his death have raised questions about whether the U psychiatrist running the study followed university ethical guidelines. They also raise questions about why the Institutional Review Board, the internal group charged with protecting people in university studies, didn't intervene.

University officials say their nationally accredited review board—a volunteer panel of 57 experts in medicine and other disciplines—works well and rigorously reviews studies. They would not talk specifically about the Markingson case to the *Pioneer Press*. A judge ruled in February [2008] that as a state agency, the university and its IRB [institutional review board] are immune from the lawsuit.

The legal ruling didn't allow questions to be explored about who's ultimately responsible for the safety of research subjects and whether the university did everything reasonable to protect Markingson from harm.

According to the U's human subjects protection guide, the IRB's first charge is "to protect human subjects involved in research at the university from inappropriate risk."

The IRB . . . has the power to shut down projects that aren't complying with safety requirements or have caused "unexpected serious harm" to subjects.

A System Based on Trust

In reality, the IRB operates largely on trust. Trust that researchers will follow the rules. Trust that people will speak up when a safety plan is violated, even if they have professional or financial pressures to stay quiet.

"It's the people who implement the plan who are responsible for protecting the subjects," said Moira Keane, the U's director of research subjects protection programs.

The IRB approves all clinical research—modifying safety rules when necessary—and samples study records every year or so to make sure its conditions are met. It also has the power to shut down projects that aren't complying with safety requirements or have caused "unexpected serious harm" to subjects.

Keane recalled four studies out of thousands at the U over the past two decades that the IRB stopped.

The lawsuit by Markingson's mother, Mary Weiss, alleged that the IRB's trust was misplaced in the so-called CAFE [comparison of atypicals in first-episode schizophrenia] study, led by Dr. Stephen Olson, a U psychiatrist.

A central allegation was whether Olson had too much power over Markingson, and too many conflicts that obscured his clinical judgment. Olson recruited Markingson into the study at the same time he served as Markingson's treating doctor and advised a Dakota County judge on whether Markingson should be committed to a psychiatric hospital.

Had the IRB followed its own guidelines, it would have discouraged Olson from recruiting his own patient. The IRB Web site states that "doctor-patient relationships between the investigator and participants should be avoided, when possible, to eliminate any power-based coercion."

Missed Opportunities

It's impossible to know whether Markingson would have killed himself if he hadn't enrolled in the research study. He was in a sensitive early stage of his schizophrenia diagnosis, during which the suicide risk is greatest. Even so, the study's rigid guidelines meant that Markingson received only one antipsychotic drug to help control his delusions.

Experts hired by Weiss' attorneys said in court depositions that the IRB missed opportunities to make the study safer.

Dr. Harrison Pope from Harvard Medical School called the IRB's role an "essential link in the chain of causation that improperly admitted Mr. Markingson into the CAFE study, improperly held Mr. Markingson within the CAFE study, prohibited effective treatment of Mr. Markingson, and thus became a substantial, proximate cause of Mr. Markingson's death."

The IRB could insist researchers turn over all complaints about their studies, which might have raised concerns in this case. Weiss had complained in letters to Olson and Dr. Charles Schulz, head of the U's Department of Psychiatry, that her son wasn't getting better and was at risk for harm. She had requested that the doctors try other treatments, even if he had to be withdrawn from the study.

The U hired its own national IRB expert to refute Pope's claims. The IRB had no legal obligation to require someone other than Olson to evaluate Markingson's competency or his ability to consent to research, said Ernest Prentice, associate vice chancellor at the University of Nebraska Medical Center.

Legal Obligations Met

Nor is there a requirement that complaints such as Weiss' letters be forwarded to the IRB unless there is some unanticipated risk. Had the IRB received complaints, it could have investigated, he said.

Weiss said she'd never heard of an IRB.

The CAFE study was fairly prominent, involving 26 academic institutions and 400 schizophrenic patients. Financed by the pharmaceutical company AstraZeneca, it was worth up to $327,000 to the U, with some of those funds going to Olson's salary and other study personnel.

U officials said the IRB acted ethically and within its obligations and federal regulations to protect human subjects in this study.

After the suicide, the IRB sought information from Olson on how Markingson consented to the study. But IRB officials said in depositions for the lawsuit that the review board never formally investigated Markingson's death.

The IRB investigates when there is evidence of misconduct. There was no evidence of that in the Markingson case, said Dr. Richard Bianco, a U physician who oversaw the U's research subjects program at the time Markingson participated in the study.

Bianco declined a *Pioneer Press* interview request. But in a court deposition, he acknowledged that the U has some 8,000 studies involving humans—research he estimated was worth about $15 million—but that the IRB doesn't track the number of people enrolled in U research, only the number of projects approved.

Bianco agreed with Keane that the IRB system operates largely on self-disclosure by researchers.

Nearly 40 percent of the psychiatry department staff . . . said they did not believe they would be protected from retaliation for blowing the whistle on a suspected violation.

Policing Themselves

The U's top research official says researchers and IRB reviewers "are aware and understand their ethical and moral obligations to do the right thing.

"If people write with concerns and issues, they will be reviewed," said Tim Mulcahy, the U's vice president of research. "If the IRB were to become aware of a suggestion of coercion or heavy handedness," he added, "we have an obligation to act promptly and very directly."

Olson declined to talk to the *Pioneer Press* about Markingson's care.

He said it would be difficult for any researcher to get away with violating research rules because they are observed by so many medical students, residents, nurses and others. However, a 2006 internal audit of the U's psychiatry department challenges the notion that those workers would speak up.

Nearly 40 percent of the psychiatry department staff responding to the auditor survey said they did not believe they would be protected from retaliation for blowing the whistle on a suspected violation in the department.

Some experts believe the nation's system of review boards is dysfunctional and in need of reform.

"We have a very haphazard way of overseeing (IRBs) and collecting data on adverse events," said Dr. Ezekiel Emanuel, bioethics chair at the Clinical Center of the National Institutes of Health and a national expert on institutional review boards.

"There's no one in America who can tell you how many people are enrolled in clinical research," he said. "No one can tell you how many people died in (ways) attributable to clinical research. No one can tell you how many people got injured, and no one can tell you over time whether the system is getting less safe."

4

Review Boards Are Inadequate to Ensure Ethical Medical Testing

Mary Beckman

Idaho-based writer Mary Beckman specializes in the life sciences and is a frequent contributor to the Journal of the National Cancer Institute.

A recent federal report shows that the US Food and Drug Administration (FDA), the federal agency responsible for approving new drugs and medical devices, does not have the ability to keep track of clinical trials, and it does not have enough staff to do proper inspections of trials. Furthermore, the FDA cannot adequately monitor the institutional review boards (IRBs) that are set up to monitor trials for ethics and safety problems. IRBs do not police clinical trials themselves; rather, they rely on the researchers to report problems, so they offer less than ideal protection for test subjects in the first place. The FDA inspects only about 1 percent of clinical trials and, without additional oversight, there is no assurance that IRBs protect study participants as they are supposed to do. The FDA needs to greatly improve its tracking of clinical trials and IRBs, conduct more inspections, and seek the legal authority to oversee all researchers involved in a study, not just the principal investigator.

Mary Beckman, "Federal Drug Agency Gets Flack About Human Subjects Protections in Clinical Trials," *Journal of the National Cancer Institute*, Vol. 100, Issue 2, January 16, 2008, pp. 90–1. Reproduced by permission.

The federal agency responsible for approving new drugs and medical devices is under fire for not doing enough to protect human subjects in research.

A recent federal report concludes that the U.S. Food and Drug Administration [FDA] lacks ways to keep track of research on people and fails to conduct enough inspections. The FDA responded by saying that human subject protection is a complicated business. While it agreed with some of the report's findings, it also said that it conducts as many inspections as it can and that even the threat of inspections ensures safe treatment of patients. Clinical investigators, on the other hand, worry that the publicity the report generated could reduce the number of patients willing to participate in a clinical trial system that they believe is safe enough and already thin on volunteers.

In the September [2008] report, the inspector general for the U.S. Department of Health and Human Services criticized the FDA for a poor showing in its efforts to protect human research subjects. The inspector general reported that the FDA has no way to keep track of all the clinical trials and review boards that monitor the trials. Also, the agency has no way to keep track of the inspections it performs or the legal authority to oversee other researchers who might be involved in clinical trials but who are not the principal investigator. The inspector general also thought that inspecting 1% of trials was inadequate. For example, the FDA has only 200 inspectors to monitor 350,000 investigators using people in research. The report recommended how the FDA could improve, including creating a database to track inspections and getting the legal authority to oversee colleagues and subordinates of principal investigators.

FDA Says Changes Already Planned

The FDA pointed out in comments to the report that the organization is already modernizing its human subject protection protocols with the kinds of databases that the report recommends. But the agency also contended that the report focused too much on inspections that are to be conducted after a trial is in progress. "Inspections are but one narrow part," the FDA responded, saying that the initial review of protocols is also important. "In order to ensure the highest degree of human subject protection, [the] FDA carefully scrutinizes all protocols submitted to the agency and will require sponsors to revise protocols as necessary, thus ensuring the greatest protection of human subjects before a clinical investigation even begins."

Research on humans is an incredibly important part of medical science and is only becoming more vital, says hematogist Edward Benz Jr., M.D., president of the Dana-Farber Cancer Institute in Boston.

Open to Dialogue

"As we learn more about the genetic basis of drugs, what a drug is useful for can only be tested in humans. The limits of animal studies are becoming more of an issue. Animals have the same genes, but their genes don't interact with drugs the same way," he says.

While recognizing that problems exist, some cancer researchers and ethicists were generally supportive of the FDA. Some say that the FDA is doing what it can and others say institutional review boards (IRBs) already do a good job of protecting human subjects. They are interested in using the report to open a broader dialogue about how to address protecting human participants in clinical studies as researchers learn more about disease in the future.

"My reaction was that it would be good if the FDA did the things that were recommended in the report," says Rebecca Dresser, J.D., a Washington University lawyer who is an expert on the FDA's regulation of drugs and devices. "But the FDA is held responsible for so many things, and it's so underfunded.

And Congress hasn't provided the money and personnel it needs to get done what it needs done."

Some researchers say that not all cancer research suffers from the issues found in the report. For example, NCI [National Cancer Institute]-designated cancer centers have put a great deal of time and money into ensuring the safety of patients, including IRBs, scientific review committees, and data safety and monitoring boards, Benz says. "We spend $10 million a year at Dana-Farber for protection of human subjects."

When researchers want FDA approval for new drugs or label changes, the agency doesn't actually monitor their human-based research itself.

Role of Institutional Review Boards

Part of the issue is that the FDA doesn't oversee most federally funded clinical cancer research—that job is left to Department of Health and Human Service's Office of Human Research Protections (OHRP). That agency requires universities, hospitals, and other research organizations to set up IRBs and register them. The OHRP is then responsible for monitoring the IRBs.

IRBs, which approve, monitor, and review human research trials, are charged with exposing potential conflicts of interest of clinicians serving as investigators, says Joseph Fins, M.D., F.A.C.P., who is chief of medical ethics at Weill Medical College of Cornell University in Ithaca, N.Y. This situation creates the potential for an adversarial dynamic. "The adversarial strategy is necessary but not sufficient" to protect subjects, he says.

IRBs are protecting subjects, but they do so based on paper, not on observing behavior, Dresser says. "IRBs rely on investigators to be honest. If unexpected problems crop up, the researcher tells the IRB. An IRB doesn't go out and police this."

While the OHRP monitors the IRBs, the FDA most often oversees private companies seeking FDA approval for their drugs. But when researchers want FDA approval for new drugs or label changes, the agency doesn't actually monitor their human-based research itself, Dresser says. They check only to see if a privately funded company has gotten IRB approval for human trials. And when the company comes back later when it's time to market its product, the FDA again looks to see if IRBs were used.

But at least U.S. research subjects have the OHRP. The bigger problem is when drug or device trials are conducted in other countries, which don't fall under OHRP jurisdiction. But companies still want to use the data for FDA approval. "The FDA is the only federal agency with oversight responsibilities in those cases. It's important to monitor those trials—some countries don't have good domestic systems for protection," Dresser said.

Medical researchers and ethicists agree that oversight is critical, but they note that even in a highly regulated environment, research carries risk.

Negative Repercussions

Benz worries that the attention given to the report will have a negative effect on getting volunteers to participate in trials. "The way the report was related in the media might have a very chilling effect on people enrolling in clinical trials," he says. "We already have a sense that people are less interested in clinical trials these days, and we don't know why."

In defending its practices, the FDA wrote that its modernization efforts will address many of the inspector general's issues but also acknowledged that because of limited resources, "human subject protection must exist in the absence of FDA's presence during the clinical trial." The agency added that rather than performing an arbitrary number of additional inspections, they need to improve upon the inspections they do conduct.

Medical researchers and ethicists agree that oversight is critical, but they note that even in a highly regulated environment, research carries risk. "IRBs are the best that anybody has been able to think of to protect people," Benz says. "But we're dealing with the unknown. You can do everything possible for safety, but research is like getting on a plane. Nothing is perfect."

Fins agrees. "We have to recognize there is risk in research. We need safeguards, though, not stasis," he says—safeguards, perhaps, that will let human cancer research keep flying high.

5

Medical Testing on Prisoners Is Unethical and Should Be Outlawed

Silja J.A. Talvi

Investigative journalist Silja J.A. Talvi is a senior editor at In These Times, *a nonprofit, independent newsmagazine. Her work also has appeared in the* Nation, Salon, Utne Reader *and the* Christian Science Monitor *among others.*

The history of medical testing on prisoners in the United States is a long and sordid story of unspeakable cruelty and unethical practices. In 1976, The National Commission for the Protection of Human Subjects of Biomedical and Behavioral Research set forth strict new research guidelines, including a section known as Subpart C that protects prisoners. Now, however, that protection is being challenged and federal officials are considering easing the rules to again allow prison research on a large scale. Not only is there insufficient federal oversight to ensure safe and ethical prison research, but experimenting on prisoners violates the Nuremburg Code, an international law regarding the treatment of people in captivity that was established in response to Nazi atrocities in World War II. The United States' history of medically abusing prisoners illustrates that medical testing in prison is unethical. It should simply be prohibited.

O ne of the most powerful movies ever to be made about the Holocaust was the 2003 made-for-TV movie, *Out of the Ashes*, which highlighted the sickening crucible faced by medical professionals held captive in the Third Reich's torture-and-killing camps.

Medical experimentation on Jewish and Roma (Gypsy) women was one of Dr. Josef Mengele's favorite forms of entertainment. In the movie, Dr. Gisella Perl (Christine Lahti) faces an ethical crisis when she is forced to comfort a young pregnant Roma woman and then stand by and watch as Mengele, the Angel of Death, marks up and slices open her stomach without the benefit of anesthesia. Mengele's sadistic detachment as he walks away from the remains of the dead woman and her fetus is agonizingly contrasted with Perl's helplessness and trauma.

Perl's story is real. Millions died, and thousands were experimented on (and then usually murdered) in the name of the Nazi "science" of eugenics. And it is because of such treatment that in 1947, the Nuremberg Code spelled out an unequivocal position on the experimentation of people in captivity: The human subject of medical experimentation "should have legal capacity to give consent . . . [and] should be so situated as to be able to exercise free power of choice, without the intervention of any element of force, fraud, deceit, duress, over-reaching or other ulterior form of constraint or coercion."

Strange thing about this country of ours—we always seem to be able to justify the "legitimate" exceptions to international law and agreements.

A Long and Sordid History

From the '40s through the early '70s, the United States officially sanctioned the use of prisoners in medical experiments, including the injection of typhoid fever, herpes, malaria, TB [tuberculosis] and a host of sexually transmitted diseases. In the name of science, doctors have dosed prisoners with LSD, placed them in extreme isolation to develop "mind control" techniques, and, in Washington State between 1963 and 1973, [ir]radiated their testicles and then sliced them open. (This last case brought about one of the few successful lawsuits by prisoners against medical experimentation.)

In 1976, things seemed to change for the better. The National Commission for the Protection of Human Subjects of Biomedical and Behavioral Research released a scathing report that led to new protections of human research subjects. The specific protections for prisoners, in a section known as Subpart C, accompanied similar protections for the disabled, children and other vulnerable populations.

Now, things may be changing again to allow for more medical experimentation on prisoners. In August [2006] the influential Institute of Medicine (IOM), presented a report, "Ethical Considerations for Research Involving Prisoners," to federal officials that recommended increasing research on prison populations. Such research, the report said, provided a way of "improving the health of prisoners and the conditions in which they live." In an August 21 [2006] editorial, *USA Today* heartily agreed.

The report also raised valid concerns about consent, safeguards, prisoner privacy and access to adequate health care while in prison. It also called for the expansion of the definition of "prisoners" to include all of the nearly 7 million persons under some form of adult correctional supervision.

Pharmaceutical companies that want to fund their own studies have no oversight body outside of what a prison or state might deem minimally necessary.

News Editorials Urge Caution

The IOM said that "respect for persons and justice should still be the basis for the conduct and regulation of prisoners today." In reaction, a *New York Times* editorial two days later observed that: "The country should move slowly on this issue. The savage and dishonorable legacy of drug testing in prison makes it imperative that any change be carried out carefully, with maximum transparency and concern for inmate safety."

But the United States has already been moving far too slowly on this issue. A 1978 federal regulation stated that prisoners can participate in federally funded research only if the "experiment poses no more than 'minimal' risk," which it defined as a "risk of physical or psychological harm that is no greater in probability and severity than that ordinarily encountered in the daily lives, or in the routine medical, dental or psychological examinations of healthy persons." While that would seem to make a certain amount of sense, federal oversight and monitoring of medical experimentation has been incredibly sloppy and disorganized, even according to those who have been responsible for that oversight. "What we've got from the regulatory standpoint is a mess," said Dr. Thomas Puglisi, the former director of compliance for the Office of Protection from Research Risks—now the Office of Human Research Protections (OHRP)—at a medical research summit in March 2001. "I couldn't say that when I worked for the federal government, but I can say that now."

Medical experimentation on prisoners in the United States never went away. Researchers just got savvier about keeping their prison studies out of the public eye.

Out of Sight, Out of Mind

And it's worth noting that the only national oversight is of clinical trials in prisons that receive federal funds. Pharmaceutical companies that want to fund their own studies have no oversight body outside of what a prison or state might deem minimally necessary. A national database of medical experimentation on prisoners does not exist. Research studies don't even always end up being published—particularly when they fail, sometimes causing serious injury or death to their human subjects.

These are among the most severe obstacles facing journalists who try to find out more about what's going on, as I discovered while pursuing a January 2002 cover story for *In These Times*.

In investigating that story, I found that the number of experimental studies on youth and adults in correctional facilities was increasing. Many of the studies clearly and egregiously violated the existing regulations on "minimal" risk to their subjects, according to FOIA [Freedom of Information Act] documents I received from the OHRP.

Simply put, medical experimentation on prisoners in the United States never went away. Researchers just got savvier about keeping their prison studies out of the public eye, often turning to pharmaceutical funding, which allows them to experiment with as little notice, oversight or intervention as possible.

Last year [2005] the OHRP Secretary's Advisory Committee on Human Research Protections (SACHRP) asked its Subpart C subcommittee (addressing prisoner safeguards) to determine whether existing regulations were still "adequate," as well as to investigate the prevalence of medical testing on prisoners.

In the internal document submitted by that subcommittee to SACHRP, more than 1,000 studies related to prisoners or incarceration came up as "hits" on a PUBMED database search. Of the 79 studies that appeared to be conducted entirely in prison settings, 63 percent had to do with sociobehavioral research revolving around substance abuse, mental illness and disease risk behaviors.

Inadequate Protections

The report noted the lack of real, centralized information on medical testing on prisoners, and added "much of the research in correctional settings is graduate student research of uncertain quality."

Medical testing in prisons should be brought to a halt—at the very least until quality prison health care for every single inmate is a reality. Genuine preventative and interventionist care for people outside of prison who cannot afford medical insurance should also be a priority.

"Before prisoners can freely make decisions about their medical care and treatment they first must have access to medical care and treatment that meets with community standards," says Paul Wright, editor of *Prison Legal News*. "Every day prisoners around the country are dying of medical neglect because they are not provided with simple, known and available medical care. It is laughable to think that somehow cutting-edge medical treatment is suddenly going to be made available to prisoners. The people carrying out the drug testing have a fiduciary duty to enrich their shareholders and employers, not provide the best medical care for prisoners."

In the current system, prisoners' lives are already endangered. In light of this country's legacy of medically abusing captive populations—and to honor the memory, intent and purpose of the creation of the Nuremberg Code—prison experimentation simply needs to come to an end.

6

Medical Testing on Prisoners Can Be Done Ethically

Institute of Medicine

The Institute of Medicine, chartered by Congress in 1970 as part of the US National Academies, advises the nation on matters of health and medicine. It was tasked by the US Department of Health and Human Services to review ethical standards for research involving prisoners and issued its review committee's report in 2007.

Although the history of medical testing on prisoners in the United States includes many past abuses, research can be done ethically if the right precautions are put in place. There are five areas in which strengthened protections would ensure research is conducted ethically: 1) define "prisoner" as a person whose freedom is restricted; 2) universally apply all protection standards in a manner that is consistent; 3) approve research proposals based on their benefits and risks for participants; 4) require that, whenever possible, participants provide input on the design and execution of studies; and 5) strengthen all the regulations and agencies that govern the treatment of prisoners participating in research studies. If medical testing is to be done on prison populations, it must always be held to the most rigorous ethical standards.

Institute of Medicine, Committee on Ethical Considerations for Revisions to DHHS Regulations for Protection of Prisoners Involved in Research, *Ethical Considerations for Research Involving Prisoners*. Washington DC: The National Academies Press, 2007, pp. 1–4, 16. Reprinted with permission from the National Academies Press, Copyright © 2000, National Academy of Sciences.

In the past 30 years, the population of prisoners in the United States has expanded more than 4.5-fold, correctional facilities are increasingly overcrowded, and more of the country's disadvantaged populations—racial minorities, women, people with mental illness, and people with communicable diseases such as human immunodeficiency virus (HIV)/acquired immune deficiency syndrome (AIDS), hepatitis C, and tuberculosis—are under correctional supervision. Because prisoners face restrictions on liberty and autonomy, limited privacy, and often inadequate health care, they require specific protections when involved in research, particularly in today's correctional settings. Given these issues, the Department of Health and Human Services (DHHS) Office for Human Research Protections (OHRP) commissioned the Institute of Medicine (IOM) to review the ethical considerations regarding research involving prisoners. The resulting analysis emphasizes five broad actions to provide prisoners involved in research with critically important protections: expand the definition of the term *prisoner*; ensure universally and consistently applied standards of protection; shift from a category-based to a risk-benefit approach to research review; update the ethical framework to include collaborative responsibility; and enhance systematic oversight of research involving prisoners.

The Prison Population

In many important ways, the U.S. correctional system is different than it was in the 1970s, when current regulations regarding prisoners as research subjects were promulgated. The total correctional population (persons in prisons, jails, probation, and parole) increased to nearly 7 million individuals between 1978 and 2004. Correctional facilities are increasingly overcrowded, and access to programs, services, and health care has not kept pace with the rising tide of prisoners. More of our country's disadvantaged populations are under correctional supervision: racial minorities, women, persons with mental illness, and persons with communicable diseases such as HIV/AIDS, hepatitis C, and tuberculosis.

Prisoners have been exploited in the past, carrying a heavier burden of the risks of research than the general population. Although the level of severity varies depending on the correctional setting, prisoners face restrictions on liberty and autonomy, limited privacy, and potentially inadequate healthcare services. These factors can be barriers to the prerequisites of ethical research, namely the acquisition of voluntary informed consent, protection of privacy, and access to adequate health care such that a choice between research participation and nonparticipation is not simply a desperate action to obtain treatment.

However, research can impart benefits. Responsible research has the potential of improving the health and wellbeing of prisoners as well as improving the conditions in which they live. Adherence to the highest ethical values, however, is critically important in designing and conducting human research involving prisoners.

"Common Rule" Regulations

Title 45 Part 46 of the Code of Federal Regulations (45 C.F.R. Part 46) contains Subpart A, the basic DHHS regulations for the protection of human research subjects, also known as the Common Rule. The Common Rule provides requirements and guidance on issues such as review by an institutional review board (IRB), informed consent by subjects, analysis of risks and benefits, protecting privacy, plus further requirements for approval of proposed research. Additional subparts of 45 C.F.R. Part 46 provide more specific protections for certain particularly vulnerable populations: pregnant women, fetuses, and neonates [newborns] (Subpart B); prisoners (Subpart C); and children (Subpart D). Subpart C (Additional Protections Pertaining to Biomedical and Behavioral Research Involving

Prisoners as Subjects), the principal focus of this report, was first finalized in 1978 and was developed in response to the *Report and Recommendations: Research Involving Prisoners* by the National Commission for the Protection of Human Subjects of Biomedical and Behavior Research (NCPHSBBR, 1976). The general stance of Subpart C is that only research that fits within four or five categories is permitted in prisoner populations.

The committee's review of current research revealed that most research involving prisoners is taking place outside the purview of Subpart C, and many prisoner studies are being conducted without IRB [institutional review board] review. There is no ethically defensible reason to exclude certain prisoners from most, if not all, human subject protections afforded by federal regulation. All of these factors point to a population that is more vulnerable and requires stronger protections than those inspired by the national commission in the 1970s.

The goal is to ensure rigorous responsible research that improves the well-being of prisoners while taking great care to protect their health, well-being, and human rights.

With these concerns in mind, the OHRP of the DHHS commissioned the IOM to review the ethical considerations in research involving prisoners as a basis for updating DHHS regulations to protect prisoners as research subjects.

The committee was charged with the following tasks:

- Consider whether the ethical bases for research with prisoners differ from those for research with nonprisoners.

- Develop an ethical framework for the conduct of research with prisoners.

- Identify considerations or safeguards necessary to ensure that research with prisoners is conducted ethically.

- Identify issues and needs for future consideration and study.

The Committee's Recommendations

The committee developed each recommendation in this report with the interests of prisoners in mind. Throughout its deliberations, the committee was well aware of the dark history of research involving prisoners and was determined not to permit the exposure of prisoners to the kind of research abuses that occurred before the national commission released its report. In this report, in fact, the committee adds further protections both by expanding the population of prisoners covered by rigorous ethical rules and by recommending additional ethical safeguards. At the same time, access to research may be critical to improve the health of prisoners and the conditions in which they live, as the committee was told by prisoners during prison site visits. The task was to strike a balance between potential benefits and risks of specific research protocols. The goal is to ensure rigorous responsible research that improves the well-being of prisoners while taking great care to protect their health, well-being, and human rights.

The setting in which prisoners are consigned must allow for the ethical conduct of research, including autonomous decision making, voluntary informed consent, and privacy protection.

The recommendations . . . will allow research, in limited circumstances, that might benefit prisoners. These limited circumstances cannot be captured by a rigid categorical approach but need to be rooted in an ethically relevant risk-benefit analysis that grapples with the balance between a need for protection and access to potentially beneficial research protocols. During the course of the committee's deliberations, five themes emerged as organizing categories for the committee's recommendations:

1. expand the definition of the term *prisoner*;

2. ensure universal, consistent ethical protection;

3. shift from a category-based to a risk-benefit approach to research review;

4. update the ethical framework to include collaborative responsibility; and

5. enhance systematic oversight of research with prisoners. . . .

Responsible, Ethical Research

The recommendations offered within this report are intended to encourage the development of a uniform system that provides critically important protections for prisoners involved in research. Research has the potential to help society better understand how to protect and promote the welfare and well-being of this large and growing segment of our society. For any research to go forward, however, it must offer more benefits than risks to prisoners, and the setting in which the prisoners are consigned must allow for the ethical conduct of research, including autonomous decision making, voluntary informed consent, and privacy protection. Strengthening systems of oversight and requiring collaboration at every level of the research process will require substantial commitments from every stakeholder. The committee acknowledges that the collaboration model, for example, will be new within most correctional settings and among many researchers. However, if research is to be supported to improve the welfare of prisoner populations, which the committee recommends, it must be done with rigorous safeguards and under a comprehensive HRPPP [human research participant protection program].

The hallmark of a decent society is to ensure humane, respectful treatment of all prisoners. Responsible, ethically appropriate research is one important aspect of the kind of society to which we aspire.

7

Medical Testing on Children Involves Unique Ethical Considerations

Donna Sylvester and Tonia Morrison

Donna Sylvester is administrative director of the Pediatric Pharmacology Research Unit and manager of the Clinical Trials Office, Training and Compliance at the Children's Hospital of Philadelphia (CHOP). Tonia Morrison is a research coordinator with the CHOP Clinical Trials Office.

Medical testing on children presents special ethical concerns that must be handled carefully. Most unique is the requirement that children in a clinical trial face no greater risk from the trial than they would face in everyday life. This is often a very difficult thing to determine, and sometimes it means that certain things simply cannot be tested in children. It is also important, even though children themselves cannot give legal consent, that their concerns are addressed fully, and that children who are old enough are allowed to assent to or express a desire to not participate in clinical trials. Researchers must take care to include the child's entire family in the process—addressing such issues as child care, accommodating school and work schedules, travel expenses, and the emotional impact of participation of the entire family—and to ensure that all of the facilities the child will need to use during the study, such as blood-draw centers, are accustomed to providing care for pediatric patients.

Pediatric clinical trials are considerably inimitable [defying imitation] compared with adult trials. Moreover, the complexities of the approval and consenting process for pediatric trials qualify them as a unique entity in the clinical research discipline. There are explicit federal regulations that an Institutional Review Board (IRB) employs to determine risk in pediatric studies. The IRB must possess the ability to be sensitive to those issues specific to the pediatric population. As a result, an IRB that comprises both clinical personnel and the lay community, who serve as a voice for children and their families, is imperative. Many characteristics of a clinical trial are scrutinized when the IRB assigns a risk category. For instance, some areas of concern are the type of study, whether the benefits to the patient are greater than the risks, whether healthy volunteers are part of the study, or whether it is a treatment or genetic study. Pediatric consent forms require readable lay language; most IRBs require that the consent form not exceed the sixth grade reading level. Since parents/guardians are customarily the consenting authority to enroll their child into a research study, it is important for them to understand what they are consenting to and why. Assent may be obtained from a child who is able to understand the trial and is of a specific age that is predetermined by the local IRB. Some parents may be content to allow their child to participate in a clinical trial for the sake of advancing medical knowledge in a specific discipline, which is considered an indirect benefit. However, this perception is notional and, ergo, the exception; most parents prefer something more concrete. Consequently, more parents/guardians are likely to enroll their child in a clinical research trial if there are obvious direct benefits.

Assessing Risk

There are concerns in pediatric trials that are unfathomable in adult trials. For instance, to recruit healthy pediatric subjects into a trial, it must be determined by the IRB that the proposed study poses no additional risk to that which would normally be encountered in everyday life. The determination may be dependent upon a number of issues; one IRB may interpret risk differently than another. Some may compare it with riding in a car, while others may compare it with crossing the street. A drive in a vehicle may be very safe in the Midwest, but risk assessment may be significantly altered if the same scenario were evaluated in a big city on the East Coast. The same holds true with crossing a street. These analogies reiterate the point that the composition of an IRB be representative of both lay and clinical staff. Lay persons are a critical component of the IRB; they address practical issues that clinicians may not have considered or perhaps have overlooked.

Phase I trials in pediatrics are important, given that they provide fundamental data for pediatric drug labeling. By providing accurate dosing to children there is a potential for more effective treatments, which may reduce hospital stays and, ultimately, insurance costs. According to the Code of Federal Regulations (CFR), pediatric trials with greater than minimal risk must confine research to children who have a condition or disorder, and the trial cannot pose any additional risks than would normally be encountered in their clinical care. Pediatric studies involving healthy subjects are generally more difficult to recruit because there is usually no direct benefit associated with this type of study.

Blood Draws Are Special Concern

From an ethical perspective, there are important facets of a phase I trial that demand consideration. Serial blood samplings, blood drawing access, and trial design are specific topics of concern. It is important that parents plainly recognize this when informed consent is obtained. Blood drawing access is another substantial issue—if it is a requisite for a two-year-old to have a peripheral intravenous (PIV) catheter placed for blood drawing, this will necessitate stabilization to avoid multiple PIVs. This procedure is replete with ethical issues. Consequently, an IRB may define the number of sticks permissible per subject. When a phase I trial is designed, blood volumes need to be considered, especially for children less than two years of age. Many sites obtain consent, but are largely ill equipped to entertain a two-year-old subject for 8–12 hours in the interest of adherence to a pharmacokinetic sampling schedule. The protocol should also be designed to address the needs of today's family. Childcare may be required, the subject may miss school, or a parent may need to take a day off from work to be with their child. Time, travel, and sundry expenses that might not be incurred if the child were not a participant in a clinical trial are vital issues that need to be broached.

Informed consent in the pediatric setting is more complex than the adult consent process. If it is an outpatient study, visit schedules and time commitments are crucial, particularly for school-age children or families with multiple siblings. Pediatric studies are expensive to conduct because in some ways you are not only consenting an individual, you are consenting an entire family unit, and any additional demands on them should be considered carefully. The subject is a patient first, particularly for disease-specific studies; clinical issues cannot be ignored. As a result, it is imperative that the clinical research team carefully assesses whether or not to approach a subject. The family may be emotionally devastated as a result of clinical circumstances, which may in turn affect the candidate's viability. This could be perceived as an auxiliary burden on the family.

Working with Families

There are also several other ethical considerations indigenous to pediatric studies. The importance of timing cannot be over-emphasized. The research team must be sensitive to the family's state of mind. Another area of concern is the clinical team caring for the child. When there are multiple clinically indicated procedures performed on a child, it is imperative that the research team be considerate of the demands already placed on the family. The research team is obliged to ensure that parents/guardians understand the procedures that are clinically indicated, and that being approached about a clinical trial may cause undue stress and confusion. With a pediatric study it is easy to overlook the child, since the parents/ guardians are usually the decision-makers. When designing a study, feasibility and logistical considerations for obtaining samples are compulsory. Scheduling blood samples around normal blood draws for clinically indicated labs or creating a pharmacokinetic study that reduces the number and volume of blood samples are essential components of a successful trial. It is imperative that the voice of a child, who may be afraid of needles or blood draws, is heard.

It is imperative to support the research subject's family but it is absolutely essential to become the subject's advocate, regardless of age.

During pediatric trials it is important to continually reiterate the procedures, schedules, and commitments. Many families may be preoccupied by the clinical issues; consequently, participating in a clinical trial may not be a priority. After enrollment many parents/guardians appreciate a study coordinator who continually reminds them of the details of the study, which may include upcoming procedures, visits and expected time commitments. It is important to be proactive with families, anticipate their needs and concerns, and allow them the opportunity to reconsider and/or withdraw at any time, or refuse procedures that may cause discomfort to their child. It is the study team's responsibility to assist the family in determining when enough is enough. It is imperative to support the research subject's family but it is absolutely essential to become the subject's advocate, regardless of age.

In summary, there are many aspects of pediatric trials that make them unique. The IRB's determination of risk sets the stage for the clinical trial. The IRB establishes how many parental/guardian signatures are required as a result of the assigned risk category. They decide whether the knowledge gained outweighs the risks. Once IRB approval is granted, it is up to the study team to uphold the determinations, and to abide by the protocol. Due to the unique nature of pediatric trials, it is essential that all of the aforementioned scenarios be considered when designing a trial.

8

Special Rules Can Provide Safeguards for Vulnerable Test Populations

David Wendler and Christine Grady

David Wendler is head of the Unit on Vulnerable Populations in the Department of Bioethics at the Warren G. Magnuson Clinical Center, National Institutes of Health (NIH). Christine Grady is the acting chief of the Department of Bioethics at the Magnuson Clinical Center, and she is head of the department's Section on Human Subjects Research.

There are several types of people who are considered vulnerable and who need extra protection when it comes to their participation in medical testing. Federal regulations include specific additional requirements for children, prisoners, and pregnant women and their fetuses. The rules also call for institutional review boards to add additional safeguards to protect disabled or vulnerable adults. The primary concern for all of these groups involves the ability of individuals to give informed consent for their participation without undue influence from others. Other groups, such as the economically disadvantaged, need not be treated as vulnerable, yet excluding such people from medical research is not ethical. Paying more attention to study design, risks, and other factors inherent in individual studies will protect study participants more effectively and fairly than simply categorizing people as vulnerable and trying to add additional measures.

David Wendler and Christine Grady, "Ethical Issues in Research with Vulnerable Populations," Department of Bioethics, National Institutes of Health, 2007. www.bioethics.nih.gov. Reproduced by permission.

Vulnerability in research involves a diminished ability to protect one's own interests, typically manifested through an inability to give informed or voluntary consent. Most children are unable to give their own voluntary, informed consent, as are some adults for various reasons. Federal regulations include specific additional requirements for research with children, prisoners, and pregnant women, and call for additional safeguards to protect vulnerable adults.

It is estimated that approximately 70 percent of medical treatments used in children have not been tested in children, even for basic safety and efficacy. This lack of evidence provides an important impetus to pursue pediatric research. A number of recent initiatives, including by the NIH [National Institutes of Health] and FDA [Food and Drug Administration], attempt to encourage and in some cases require pediatric research. With the expected increase in pediatric research comes increased emphasis on the need to ensure the children who participate in clinical research receive appropriate protection.

The [NIH] Department [of Bioethics]'s efforts with regard to research on children began with a survey of 188 IRB [institutional review board] chairpersons around the country. The federal regulations direct IRBs to categorize the risks of pediatric research in comparison to the risks children face in daily life. Specifically, a research intervention qualifies as minimal risk provided its risks do not exceed the risks children face in daily life or during the performance of routine procedures. Our survey found wide variation in how IRB chairpersons apply this minimal risk standard with, for example, 48 percent of chairpersons categorizing an MRI [magnetic resonance imaging] as minimal risk and 44 percent categorizing the very same procedure as more than minimal risk. We speculated that, in the absence of systematic data on the risks children face in daily life, IRB chairpersons might be relying on personal judgment to assess the risks of pediatric research. Extensive psychological research establishes, however, that reliance on personal judgment or intuition, in the absence of systematic data, is an unreliable method of risk assessment.

Assessing the Risks for Children

In an effort to develop systematic data, we followed this survey with an extensive review of existing data bases on the risks children face in daily life. These data provide IRBs with a baseline for systematically assessing whether research risks exceed the risks children face in daily life. Because the risks children face in daily life often are of different types compared to the risks posed by research procedures, IRBs cannot simply compare the risks of research participation directly to the risks of daily life. For example, airway intubation as part of a research study poses some risk of airway abrasion whereas daily life poses essentially no risk of airway abrasion to ordinary children. To facilitate implementation of the minimal risk standard, we developed a systematic method, which we call 'comparative' analysis, for comparing different types of risks. This approach divides the potential harms children face in daily life into five levels of severity, from negligible to catastrophic, and quantifies the chances that children will experience a harm at each respective level from the activities of daily life. This approach provides IRBs with a systematic method to determine whether research procedures pose greater than minimal risk.

Our initial survey evaluated how IRB chairpersons apply the federal minimal risk standard to hypothetical examples. Development of the comparative analysis method put us in a position to address this limitation by assessing how IRBs apply the minimal risk standard in practice, to actual clinical research studies. In particular, we applied the comparative analysis method to studies submitted to OHRP [Office of Human Research Protections] for possible approval in category 407 of the regulations. This analysis suggests misapplication of the minimal risk standard is widespread, underscoring the need to develop systematic methods, such as the comparative analysis, and assess them in practice, for implementing the federal minimal risk standard.

Federal Standard Is Minimal Risk

The federal regulations allow children to be enrolled in research that poses greater than minimal risk and offers no prospect for direct benefit when the risks do not exceed a 'minor' increase over minimal risk. Although this standard has been in place for over 20 years, there have been few systematic attempts to define what constitutes a minor increase over minimal risk. We have argued that the most widely cited approach, endorsed by [experts Charles] Weijer and [Benjamin] Freedman, suffers from a number of fatal flaws. Most importantly, this approach is limited to psychological risks. We proposed instead that a 'minor increase' over minimal risk should be understood as referring to the risks in the daily lives of children who face greater than average, but nonetheless socially acceptable risks, such as the risks faced by children who work on family farms.

Children should be deemed capable of assent when they can make their own decisions regarding research participation.

Our survey of IRB chairpersons also revealed wide variation in implementation of the "assent" requirement, the only requirement in the federal regulations to address the extent to which children should have a say in whether they are enrolled in research. Previously, it had been widely assumed that most IRBs regard children as being capable of assent at the age of 7, a threshold that has been endorsed by the National Commission [for the Protection of Human Subjects of Biomedical and Behavioral Research] and American Academy of Pediatrics.

Our survey found IRBs use a range of ages from as low as 5 years to as high as 14 years. We also found that almost half of IRBs do not use an age cutoff at all, but leave this determination to investigators' clinical judgment.

These data highlighted the need to develop systematic guidelines on the age at which children are capable of assent. For this purpose, we considered first the purpose of soliciting the assent of children. This analysis suggests children should be deemed capable of assent when they can make their own decisions regarding research participation. We evaluated existing data on cognitive development. On this basis, we argued that the assent threshold should be set at approximately age 14. This analysis also suggested that it is a mistake to rely exclusively on the assent requirement for pediatric research since this requirement does not provide any reason to respect the dissent of children deemed incapable of assent. To address this concern, we have argued that investigators also should respect the sustained dissent of all children.

The Impact of Research

As a result of its work on pediatric research ethics, consultation from members of the department has been requested by two IOM [Institute of Medicine] committees working on pediatric research ethics. The department's work on minimal risk was cited in the IOM committee report on pediatric clinical research. The department also was asked to write the principal background paper for the report of the IOM committee on housing research with children. The department's work on minimal risk and assent have been widely cited and presented at numerous conferences.

The federal regulations on pediatric research, like many guidelines around the world, focus on 'direct' benefits. On this approach, the risks to which children are exposed in the research context can be compensated by direct benefits, but not by indirect benefits. Unfortunately, there has been little examination of this crucial concept. The most systematic analysis comes from Nancy King, who defines a direct benefit as one that is the result of the intervention being tested in the study in question. We are currently working on an analysis which suggests King's account is unnecessarily restrictive. Direct benefits are better understood as benefits that result from the interventions necessary to answer the scientific question posed by the protocol.

We also are developing a practical method IRBs can use to assess the risks of pediatric research. The need for such a method was highlighted by our survey, which found that many IRB chairpersons do not understand what constitutes a "prospect" of direct benefit, while others were implementing this requirement inappropriately, assuming that any chance of direct benefit was sufficient for a protocol to qualify as offering a prospect of direct benefit. Finally, recent media coverage has focused on the ethical issues concerned with enrolling in research children who are wards of the state. The department has undertaken an analysis of the present regulations for wards, which suggests several modifications should be adopted to ensure appropriate protection for this especially vulnerable population. In particular, the scope of the responsibility of advocates should be clarified and expanded, and wards should be enrolled in research only when there is a compelling scientific reason why the study needs to enroll them.

Instead of labeling whole groups of people vulnerable, other aspects of research such as the particular design, the inherent risks, the level of uncertainty, etc. should warrant "special scrutiny."

Research with Vulnerable Adults

Many groups of adults have been described as vulnerable, to the extent that it can be difficult to determine who is not vulnerable, thereby diminishing the possibility of meaningful additional protections. To take one example, guidelines published by the Council of International Organizations of Medical Sciences (CIOMS) include junior or subordinate members of a hierarchical group, such as "medical and nursing students, subordinate hospital and laboratory personnel, employees of pharmaceutical companies, and members of the armed forces or police . . . the elderly . . . residents of nursing homes, people receiving welfare benefits or social assistance and other poor people and the unemployed, people in emergency rooms, some ethnic and racial minority groups, homeless persons, nomads, refugees or displaced persons, prisoners, patients with incurable disease, individuals who are politically powerless, and members of communities unfamiliar with modern medical concepts" as vulnerable.

In addition to including too many groups, current concepts of vulnerability are applied to whole groups of people, without distinguishing between individuals in a group who might truly have compromised capacity to protect their own interests from those who do not. Considering all poor people, pregnant women, members of ethnic or racial minorities, and people with terminal illness as inherently vulnerable has been particularly controversial. An individual's needs for special protections in the research context may depend more on personal factors, characteristics of the research and the research environment, and available alternatives, than merely on that person's membership in a particular sociodemographic group.

The federal regulations for clinical research stipulate that IRBs should include additional protections for individuals who are deemed vulnerable, or exclude them. Yet, there has been little analysis or recommendation in the literature on what constitutes appropriate protections in this regard. The existing regulations provide additional explicit requirements for three groups: prisoners, pregnant women and fetuses, and children. However, the National Commission's recommendations for research with cognitively impaired adults were never adopted. This gap is especially troubling because existing regulations rely heavily on the protections afforded by informed consent, possibly leaving adults who cannot consent without adequate safeguards.

There is little justification for routinely excluding the economically disadvantaged from research or categorically considering them vulnerable.

Special Scrutiny

The Department's work in this area began in collaboration with members of the Consortium to Examine Clinical Research Ethics (CECRE established in 2001 by the Doris Duke Charitable Foundation) examining the concept of vulnerability and critiquing current understandings and use of the concept. We argued that with a few exceptions (such as children) instead of labeling whole groups of people vulnerable, other aspects of research such as the particular design, the inherent risks, the level of uncertainty, etc. should warrant "special scrutiny".

Building on this work, we have undertaken several projects related to understanding vulnerability of the socioeconomically disadvantaged in research. Members of the department undertook an analysis of the inclusion in research of the uninsured, arguing that categorical exclusion was unfair but that targeting may also be unfair. Working with NIH collaborators from NIAMS [National Institute of Arthritis and Musculskeletal and Skin Diseases] and the NIH Clinical Center, we began to explore issues related to vulnerability in the uninsured and economically disadvantaged with the core community group of the Health Partnership Program formed by NIAMS and the Upper Cardozo Clinic in Washington DC. Using vignettes, we explored issues related to exploitation, vulnerability and trust with this core group. After a small series of individual interviews and additional meetings with the HPP [human participant protection] core community group, we are beginning an empirical study of research participants at the Cardozo Clinic to better understand their views about research and vulnerability.

Concomitantly, we examined common arguments and concerns about vulnerability of the economically disadvantaged, concluding that there is little justification for routinely excluding the economically disadvantaged from research or categorically considering them vulnerable.

Individuals who cannot consent should not be enrolled unless necessary, even when the research offers them the prospect of direct benefit.

Some Cultures Distrust Research

It has been widely assumed that individuals from minority groups in the United States, especially African Americans, are less willing to participate in health research compared to non-Hispanic whites. The literature describes this lack of willingness as based on prevalent distrust among African Americans in research and the research establishment, evolving from a legacy of abuse. This assumption has led many to assume that any efforts to increase minority participation in research must first focus on individuals' attitudes. Despite the prevalence of this view, there has been no systematic assessment of whether individuals from minority groups are less willing to participate, when eligible and invited. We conducted a systematic analysis of the published literature to assess this view. Our analysis suggests, contrary to the common view, that individuals from minority groups are as willing as whites to participate in health research.

The Department's work on identifying appropriate protections for vulnerable individuals began by arguing that enrollment in research of individuals who are in fact unable to provide informed consent poses increased moral risks, compared to the enrollment of individuals who can consent. By analogy to individuals who face increased physical risks, for example, individuals with decreased kidney function, this conclusion implies that individuals who cannot consent should not be enrolled unless there are compelling reasons to enroll them. We have labeled this safeguard the "necessity" requirement.

Is Exclusion Discrimination?

There has been much debate over whether adults who cannot consent should be enrolled in research that offers them the prospect of direct benefit. Some argue that such a restriction represents discrimination against a vulnerable group; others argue that these individuals deserve additional protection in the research setting. Our analysis of the necessity requirement suggested that these limitations are justified not on the grounds that they protect the interests of specific individuals, but that they minimize the aggregate risks of the research. This analysis suggests individuals who cannot consent should not be enrolled unless necessary, even when the research offers them the prospect of direct benefit.

We next conducted a systematic assessment of the existing recommendations for research with cognitively impaired adults. Based on this work, we developed a set of core safeguards for this type of research. In this work, we argued that the necessity requirement provides better and more appropriate protection than the widely endorsed "subject's condition" requirement.

One protection that has been advocated by a number of groups is the requirement that adults who cannot consent should be enrolled in research only when they have completed a formal research advance directive. To assess this requirement, we evaluated the attitudes of participants in research studying individuals at increased risk of developing Alzheimer disease. The results suggested that, in the absence of a formal advance directive, these individuals were willing to allow their family members to decide whether to enroll them in research should they lose the ability to make these decisions for themselves.

The Effect of Advance Directives

This survey also attempted to assess the completion rate of research advance directives by measuring how many individuals completed a research advance directive when it was provided to them. The respondents had just completed a survey of the importance of research advance directives, and the vast majority expressed support for their use. Yet, less than one in five actually completed a research advance directive. These data may not track completion rates in clinical practice. To address this limitation, we assessed research participants who come to the NIH Clinical Center which enquires whether all inpatients have an advance directive, provides written information on advance directives and encourages individuals to complete an advance directive. We found that only 11 percent of inpatients completed a research advance directive. These data provide further evidence that requiring a formal advance directive for adults who cannot consent for themselves would block many individuals from participating in research, including those who had expressed an interest in such research and were willing to allow their family member to enroll them. We conclude that a research advance directive should be understood as a recommendation, not a requirement and in the absence of a formal advance directive, family members should be allowed to make research decisions. In addition, to implement the substituted judgment standard, as the risk/benefit profile of research becomes less favorable to participants, more evidence should be required of their own preferences about participation.

Impact of Research

The Department's work on research with vulnerable adults, adults who cannot consent for themselves, and the role of advance directives in such research has been widely cited. We have received numerous requests from institutions and IRBs around the country, who use our proposed guidelines on research with adults who cannot consent to inform their policies and practices. Since it publication this year [2007], our assessment of minorities' willingness to participate in research has generated a great deal of interest, including presentation at a DHHS [Department of Health and Human Services] conference on research with minority populations. This work was also the centerpiece for an office of minority health workshop on increasing minority participation in clinical research.

The NIH Clinical Center was one of the first research institutions in the country to adopt an explicit policy regulating research with cognitively impaired adults. Since adoption of the policy almost 20 years ago there has been an evolution in thinking on the topic. The department is currently working with the Clinical Center's ethics committee to develop a revision of this policy to reflect in practice the recommendations we have made in this area. Second, we have been conducting research on decision making by surrogates. This work reveals that almost all the work to date in this area has been in the context of clinical care. Future studies will assess the nature of surrogate decision making in the research setting. Research participants at the Cardozo Clinic will be interviewed in Spanish or English to ascertain their views about research, vulnerability, exploitation, and related concepts. The department plans to continue its work examining the meaning and limitations of the concept of vulnerability, especially in economically disadvantaged populations both domestically and internationally.

9

Using Animals for Medical Testing Is Unethical and Unnecessary

People for the Ethical Treatment of Animals (PETA)

People for the Ethical Treatment of Animals (PETA) is the largest animal rights organization in the world, with more than two million members and supporters.

Millions of animals suffer and die needlessly every year in the United States as they become subjects for medical testing and other horrible experiments. Although most people assume such activity is necessary to advance medical science, in reality it does very little to improve human health. The results of animal testing do not directly transfer to humans, and such results can also be easily manipulated. Most countries around the world, including the United States, have few or inadequte laws to regulate what can be done to research animals, and even though there may be non-animal research methods available, there are no laws that require researchers to use them instead. Using animals for medical testing is both unethical and unnecessary. True medical progress demands adopting nonviolent methods of scientific investigation.

Each year, more than 100 million animals—including mice, rats, frogs, dogs, cats, rabbits, hamsters, guinea pigs, monkeys, fish, and birds—are killed in U.S. laboratories for chemical, drug, food, and cosmetics testing; biology lessons; medical

"Animal Experiments: Overview," People for the Ethical Treatment of Animals (PETA), 2011. www.peta.org. Reproduced by permission.

training; and curiosity-driven experimentation. Before their deaths, some are forced to inhale toxic fumes, others are immobilized in restraint devices for hours, some have holes drilled into their skulls, and others have their skin burned off or their spinal cords crushed. In addition to the torment of the actual experiments, animals in laboratories are deprived of everything that is natural and important to them—they are confined to barren cages, socially isolated, and psychologically traumatized. The thinking, feeling animals who are used in experiments are treated like nothing more than disposable laboratory equipment.

While a Pew Research poll found 43 percent of adults surveyed oppose the use of animals in scientific research, other surveys suggest that those who do accept animal experimentation do so only because they believe it to be necessary for medical progress. The reality is that the majority of animal experiments do not contribute to improving human health, and the value of the role that animal experimentation plays in most medical advances is questionable.

The results of animal experiments can be variable and easily manipulated.

In an article published in *The Journal of the American Medical Association*, researchers warned that "patients and physicians should remain cautious about extrapolating the finding of prominent animal research to the care of human disease . . . poor replication of even high-quality animal studies should be expected by those who conduct clinical research."

Diseases that are artificially induced in animals in a laboratory are never identical to those that occur naturally in human beings. And because animal species differ from one another biologically in many significant ways, it becomes even more unlikely that animal experiments will yield results that will be correctly interpreted and applied to the human condition in a meaningful way.

Unreliable Results

For example, according to former National Cancer Institute Director Dr. Richard Klausner, "We have cured mice of cancer for decades, and it simply didn't work in humans." And although at least 85 HIV/AIDS vaccines have been successful in nonhuman primate studies, as of 2010, every one of nearly 200 preventive and therapeutic vaccine trials has failed to demonstrate benefit to humans. In one case, an AIDS vaccine that was shown to be effective in monkeys failed in human clinical trials because it did not prevent people from developing AIDS, and some believe that it made them *more* susceptible to the disease. According to a report in the British newspaper *The Independent,* one conclusion from the failed study was that "testing HIV vaccines on monkeys before they are used on humans, does not in fact work."

Ninety-two percent of drugs—those that have been tested on animals and in vitro—do not make it through Phase 1 of human clinical trials (the initial studies that determine reaction, effectiveness, and side effects of doses of a potential drug).

In addition, the results of animal experiments can be variable and easily manipulated. Research published in the journal *Annals of Internal Medicine* revealed that universities commonly exaggerate findings from animal experiments conducted in their laboratories and "often promote research that has uncertain relevance to human health and do not provide key facts or acknowledge important limitations." One study of media coverage of scientific meetings concluded that news stories often omit crucial information and that "the public may be misled about the validity and relevance of the science presented." Because experimenters rarely publish results of failed animal studies, other scientists and the public do not have ready access to information on the ineffectiveness of animal experimentation.

Despite the countless animals killed each year in laboratories worldwide, most countries have grossly inadequate regulatory measures in place to protect animals from suffering.

Funding and Accountability

Through their taxes, charitable donations, and purchases of lottery tickets and consumer products, members of the public are ultimately the ones who—knowingly or unknowingly—fund animal experimentation. One of the largest sources of funding comes from publicly funded government granting agencies such as the U.S. National Institutes of Health (NIH). Approximately 40 percent of NIH-funded research involves experimentation on nonhuman animals, and in 2009, the NIH budgeted nearly $29 billion for research and development. In addition, many charities—including the March of Dimes, the American Cancer Society, and countless others—use donations to fund experiments on animals. Visit HumanSeal.org to find out which charities do and which do not fund research on animals.

Despite the vast amount of public funds being used to underwrite animal experimentation, it is nearly impossible for the public to obtain current and complete information regarding the animal experiments that are being carried out in their communities or funded with their tax dollars. State open-records laws and the U.S. Freedom of Information Act can be used to obtain documents and information from state institutions, government agencies, and other federally funded facilities, but private companies, contract labs, and animal breeders are exempt. In many cases, institutions that are subject to open-records laws fight vigorously to withhold information about animal experimentation from the public.

Oversight and Regulation

Despite the countless animals killed each year in laboratories worldwide, most countries have grossly inadequate regulatory measures in place to protect animals from suffering and distress or to prevent them from being used when a non-animal approach is readily available. In the U.S., the most commonly used species in laboratory experiments (mice, rats, birds, reptiles, and amphibians) are specifically exempted from even the minimal protections of the federal Animal Welfare Act (AWA). Laboratories that use only these species are not required by law to provide animals with pain relief or veterinary care, to search for and consider alternatives to animal use, to have an institutional committee review proposed experiments, or to be inspected by the U.S. Department of Agriculture (USDA) or any other entity. Experimenters don't even have to count the mice and rats they kill. Some estimates indicate that as many as 800 U.S. laboratories are not subject to federal laws and inspections because they experiment exclusively on mice, rats, and other animals whose use is unregulated.

Even animals who are covered by the law can be burned, shocked, poisoned, isolated, starved, forcibly restrained, addicted to drugs, and brain damaged—no procedures or experiments . . . are prohibited by law.

As for the approximately 9,000 facilities that the USDA does regulate (of which about 1,000 are designated for "research"), only 99 USDA inspectors are employed to oversee their operations. Reports over a span of 10 years concluded that even the minimal standards set forth by the AWA are not being met by these facilities. In 2000, a USDA survey of the agency's laboratory inspectors revealed serious problems in numerous areas, including "the search for alternatives [and] review of painful procedures." A September 2005 audit report issued by the USDA Office of the Inspector General (OIG) found ongoing "problems with the search for alternative research, veterinary care, review of painful procedures, and the researchers' use of animals." The OIG report estimated that experimenters failed to search for alternatives at almost one-third of facilities.

Even animals who are covered by the law can be burned, shocked, poisoned, isolated, starved, forcibly restrained, addicted to drugs, and brain-damaged—no procedures or experiments, regardless of how trivial or painful they may be, are prohibited by law. When valid non-animal research methods are available, no law requires experimenters to use such methods instead of animals.

The Way Forward

Human clinical, population, and *in vitro* studies are critical to the advancement of medicine; even animal experimenters need them—if only to confirm or reject the validity of their experiments. However, research with human participants and other non-animal methods does require a different outlook, one that is creative and compassionate and embraces the underlying philosophy of ethical science. Animal experimenters artificially induce diseases; clinical investigators study people who are already ill or who have died. Animal experimenters want a disposable "research subject" who can be manipulated as desired and killed when convenient; clinicians must do no harm to their patients or study participants. Animal experimenters face the ultimate dilemma—knowing that their artificially created "animal model" can never fully reflect the human condition, while clinical investigators know that the results of their work are directly relevant to people.

Human health and well-being can also be promoted by adopting nonviolent methods of scientific investigation and concentrating on the prevention of disease before it occurs, through lifestyle modification and the prevention of further environmental pollution and degradation. The public needs to become more aware and more vocal about the cruelty and inadequacy of the current research system and must demand that its tax dollars and charitable donations not be used to fund experiments on animals.

10

Using Animals for Medical Testing Is Both Ethical and Essential

Foundation for Biomedical Research

The Foundation for Biomedical Research is the nation's oldest and largest organization dedicated to improving human and animal health by promoting public understanding, respect, and support for humane and responsible animal research in scientific and medical discovery.

Animals that are used for medical testing play a vital role in scientific progress. From testing drugs to helping doctors develop new surgical procedures, lab animals remain a key part in developing new treatments for humans and animals alike. Much of the opposition to animal testing is based on misinformation and emotional arguments. The reality is that government regulations ensure that lab animals are humanely treated and that experiments are conducted ethically. Researchers who use live animals in their studies are committed to using fewer animals, using alternative methods when at all possible, and working to perfect research techniques so that animals are not subjected to anything less than the highest standards of humane treatment. Knowing that research animals are treated respectfully, responsibly, and humanely strengthens the public's understanding and respect for the essential role that lab animals play in biomedical research.

Foundation for Biomedical Research, *Fact v. Myth About the Essential Need for Animals in Medical Research*. Washington, DC: Foundation for Biomedical Research, 2008. Reproduced by permission.

Whether they're assisting in search and rescue operations, working with police and fire investigators to solve a crime, or living in an educational setting, animals make our world safer, healthier, and happier.

Many Americans form deeply satisfying, joyful relationships with their companion animals and often consider them family members. The visually and hearing impaired, as well as those living with epilepsy, look to animals for invaluable assistance with daily living. And chronic care facilities increasingly rely on animals to provide loving companionship for the sick and the lonely. A growing number of employers even welcome dogs, cats, and rabbits into the workplace because they believe the animals enhance employee performance and morale.

Like service animals, lab animals also play a heroic and vitally important role in medical progress. That's because research is the foundation for all medical science, and lab animals are the foundation of that research.

Biomedical research involving lab animals has played a vital role in virtually every major medical advance of the last century.

Genomics, stem cell research, therapeutic cloning, and biotechnology all offer tremendous hope for the future of health and healing. Advances in surgical techniques and procedures, such as organ transplantation, as well as development of remarkable new drugs and medical devices hold great promise for reducing and eliminating infectious diseases like AIDS and hepatitis, and for treating and curing deadly diseases like cancer and re-growing damaged spinal cord nerves to reverse paralysis.

Medical progress, for human health and animal health, requires lab animal research because there is no complete replacement for the whole living system. In recent years, a number of non-animal procedures have been developed for certain types of testing, and that number continues to grow.

The Three Rs

Indeed, whether they are studying human health or animal health, scientists place a high priority on "The Three Rs"— reduction, replacement, and refinement. Here in the United States, our scientific and medical research communities are committed to supporting the development of techniques that promote humane animal research by:

- Reducing the number of animals needed in any given study

- Replacing animals with other models whenever possible

- Refining procedures to ensure the most humane treatment possible using the fewest number of animals to yield valid results

Still, it isn't always easy to reconcile our love and appreciation for animals and the essential need for research. Knowing that lab animals are treated respectfully, responsibly and as humanely as possible strengthens our understanding—as does separating the facts from the myths.

Biomedical research involving lab animals has played a vital role in virtually every major medical advance of the last century. Practically every present-day protocol for the prevention, control and cure of disease, and relief of pain, is based on knowledge attained—directly or indirectly—through research with animals. Physicians and scientists overwhelmingly agree that animal systems provide invaluable and irreplaceable insights into human systems because there are striking similarities between the genetic and physiological systems of animals and humans.

While medical and scientific advances achieved through research with animals are frequently *supplemented* by knowledge obtained through non-animal methods—such as computer models, mathematical models, cell and tissue cultures, clinical observation, and epidemiology—these 'alternative' methods serve only as adjuncts to basic animal research.

As yet, there is no complete alternative to biomedical research with animals. There is still an essential need to develop surgical procedures, test drugs, medical devices, and other promising treatments on some animals before they are tested on humans since even the most sophisticated technology cannot mimic the complex cellular interactions that occur in a living system.

However, prospects are favorable for reducing the use of animals in the area of product development and testing. And conceivably, the day may come when animal research is no longer necessary.

There is absolutely no evidence to support the claim that millions of dogs and cats are taken from homes and shelters and sold to laboratories.

By the Numbers

Practically *all* research animals are rodents—mice and rats—bred for this purpose. Dogs, cats, and non-human primates *together* account for less than one half of one percent of the total, and their number has declined for more than 25 years. Since 1979, the number of dogs and cats needed in animal research has declined by more than 50 percent. The number of primates needed represents 0.2 percent and has remained relatively constant—in the 50,000 per year range—for the past decade.

There is an essential need for canines in the study of lung and heart disease as their cardiovascular and respiratory systems closely match those of humans.

Nobel Prize–winning research on the immunological basis for organ rejection was done with dogs.

Similarly, Nobel Prize–winning research with felines has contributed enormously to our understanding of eye disorders such as strabismus (or "cross-eye") and amblyopia, a serious visual impairment that can cause blindness in one or both eyes.

There is an essential need for non-human primates, mainly rhesus monkeys, in the study of arteriosclerosis, reproductive disorders, Alzheimer's, Parkinson's disease, and infectious diseases such as viral hepatitis and AIDS.

Despite frequent, unsubstantiated accusations to the contrary, there is absolutely no evidence to support the claim that millions of dogs and cats are taken from homes and shelters and sold to laboratories. In fact, scientists neither *need* nor *want* to do research on pets.

According to the United States Department of Agriculture (USDA), one of several government agencies overseeing the use of animals in medical research, 66,314 dogs and 21,637 cats were needed for biomedical research in 2006. The vast majority of these animals were bred specifically for research. The remainder were acquired directly from the "death row" of animal pounds or purchased from a USDA-licensed and regulated dealer.

The Foundation for Biomedical Research recommends that all companion animals wear collars and identification tags at all times. Tags, implanted microchips, and even tattoos can help to re-unite a lost cat or dog with its family.

Government Regulations

The USDA has set forth federal regulations governing the care and use of animals in biomedical research that are considered more extensive than those covering human research subjects. The Animal Welfare Act sets high standards of care for research animals with regard to their housing, feeding, cleanliness, ventilation, and medical needs. It also requires the use of anesthesia or analgesic drugs for potentially painful procedures and during post-operative care.

Most importantly, research institutions are required—by law—to establish an Institutional Animal Care and Use Committee (IACUC) to oversee their work with animals. IACUCs require researchers to justify their need for animals; select the most appropriate species and study the fewest number of animals possible to answer a specific question.

The U.S. Public Health Service (PHS) Act requires that all institutions receiving research funds from the National Institutes of Health, the Food and Drug Administration, or the Centers for Disease Control adhere to the standards set out in the *Guide for the Care and Use of Laboratory Animals*. Under the PHS policy, institutions must follow detailed animal care recommendations and establish an IACUC to ensure that all animals are treated responsibly and humanely.

The vast majority of biomedical research does not result in significant discomfort or distress to research animals.

Researchers Act with Compassion

For humane, compassionate, and scientific reasons, researchers are deeply concerned about the condition of the animals they study. This is not a controversial position—there is no constituency for inhumane or irresponsible treatment. Poor care results in unreliable research data. For results to be valid, animal subjects must be in good condition and appropriately healthy. Also, pain and distress are thought to have a negative impact on the immune system so researchers are careful to protect their animals from undue stress.

In the words of the esteemed Dr. Michael E. DeBakey, Chancellor Emeritus of the Baylor College of Medicine and Director of the DeBakey Heart Center: "These scientists, veterinarians, physicians, surgeons, and others who do research in animal laboratories are as much concerned about the care of the animals as anyone can be. Their respect for the dignity of life and compassion for the sick and disabled, in fact, is what motivated them to search for ways of relieving the pain and suffering caused by diseases."

It is well recognized that animals have been indispensable to the cause of medical and scientific research. We have a moral duty to provide them the best care and treatment possible.

The vast majority of biomedical research does not result in significant discomfort or distress to research animals.

The 2006 USDA Annual Report reveals that 57 percent of all research procedures with animals involved no more than slight or momentary pain or distress (i.e., an injection). Thirty-eight percent of the research procedures employed anesthesia and post-operative painkillers.

In seven percent of the procedures, neither anesthesia nor pain medication could be used, as they would have interfered with research results. However, when this is the case, discomfort is minimized as much as possible.

Stem Cell Research

Promising medical treatments are on the horizon, thanks to the tremendous capabilities of stem cells, but stem cell treatments must first demonstrate safety and efficacy in animal models before they can be introduced in humans. Stem cells have the potential to regenerate cells, tissues and organs, and to serve as delivery tools of important growth factors. Neural stem cells have been shown to deliver enzymes to brain cells in rats, penetrating the blood-brain barrier, and pointing to a potential treatment for Alzheimer's. Scientist are now developing drugs to regulate the actions of stem cells once they have been implanted, to be sure that they reproduce at the proper rate and that they differentiate into the right kind of cells.

Stem cells also allow close examination of the stages of cell and tissue development, and the origins of abnormalities. In fact, with further study, stem cells may be capable of replicating tissues and organs with such precision that fewer animal models would be required for certain types of research. However, there is still much that is unknown about stem cells and how they can best be used to treat diseases and disorders. It is critical, therefore, that scientist have the ability to explore all avenues of stem cell research to most fully benefit human and animal health.

The vast majority of Americans support improving human and animal health through the responsible and humane use of animals in medical and scientific research.

Practically all biomedical research with lab animals advances veterinary medicine as well as human medicine and helps animals live longer, happier, and healthier lives. Dozens of diseases, affecting both humans and animals, are prevented through the administration of vaccines. Many other conditions are successfully treated, in both humans and animals, with antibiotics.

From asthma to epilepsy, from high blood pressure and heart disease to cancer, people and their pets share a myriad of diseases and therapies. And thanks to animal research, effective new drugs have been designed, sophisticated medical devices have been developed and remarkable surgical procedures have been perfected—for human and veterinary medical care.

Public Support

The vast majority of Americans support improving human and animal health through the responsible and humane use of animals in medical and scientific research. And most Americans love animals. The two concepts are not mutually exclusive—when you know the facts. Though it isn't easy to reconcile our love and appreciation for animals and the essential need for animal research, knowing that the animals are treated respectfully, responsibly, and as humanely as possible, strengthens our understanding and respect for animal research.

Those who seek to end animal research—either because they choose to reject its well established validity and usefulness or because they believe the life of a rat is equal in importance to the life of a child—have gone to shocking lengths to subvert medical and scientific progress. University laboratories have been broken into, animals stolen and years of precious research data destroyed. Though many animal rights organizations refuse to condemn such criminal behaviors, law-abiding Americans have not, do not now, and will not in the future tolerate violent and radical activist campaigns against the biomedical research community.

11

Genetic Testing Necessitates New Ethical Considerations

North Carolina Association for Biomedical Research

The North Carolina Association for Biomedical Research is a nonprofit membership-based organization that promotes public understanding and support for bioscience research.

Every human has a unique genetic fingerprint called DNA that is made up of the genes that determine how the body looks and functions. Genetic testing looks for abnormalities in a person's genes that can indicate an inherited disposition toward a disease or disorder. Although genetic testing can improve lives by providing important health information, it also raises significant ethical concerns about how the results are interpreted, how decisions are made about the relative determination of quality of life, the emotional challenges presented by the testing process and results, and whether the test results could provoke discrimination against individuals by insurance companies, employers, and even parents. People who pursue genetic testing typically receive counseling to help them consider such ethical issues. A special advisory committee provides the federal government's Department of Health and Human Services with policy advice about the complex medical, ethical, legal, and social issues raised by genetic testing.

Each person has a unique set of chemical blueprints that determines how his or her body looks and functions. These blueprints are contained in a complex chemical called deox-

North Carolina Association for Biomedical Research, "Issue Brief—Genetic Testing," North Carolina's Bioscience Clearinghouse, October 2006, 1–6. Reproduced by permission.

yribonucleic acid (DNA), a long, spiral-shaped molecule found inside each cell. Specific segments of DNA that contain the instructions for making specific body proteins are called genes. As of April 2006, scientists believe human DNA carries between 20,000 and 25,000 genes.

Some genes direct the formation of structural proteins, which eventually determine physical features such as brown eyes or curly hair. Other genes provide instructions for the body to produce important chemicals called enzymes—proteins that act as natural catalysts for the chemical reactions occurring within our bodies. Even a small error within the DNA structure sometimes can mean serious problems for the entire body.

The term *genetic testing* covers an array of techniques, including analysis of DNA, RNA (ribonucleic acid) and proteins designed to look for abnormalities in a person's genes or the presence or absence of key proteins whose production is directed by specific genes. Abnormalities in either case could indicate an inherited disposition toward a disorder. This testing of an individual's DNA is performed by taking cells from a sample of blood or, occasionally, from other body fluids or tissues.

With increasing frequency, scientists are discovering associations between particular gene mutations and disease. More than 1,000 genetic tests now are available, and scientists are predicting that, with the innovative technologies being developed, genetic testing one day will give us the ability to analyze a person's complete DNA sequence, thereby allowing doctors to determine the specific disease-associated genes each person carries.

Genes are found inside the cells of every organism, from bacteria to humans. Genetic information is encoded and transmitted from generation to generation through DNA, which is organized within cells into structures called chromosomes. Genes are found in specific segments along the length of human DNA, neatly packaged within these chromosomes. Every human cell contains 46 chromosomes, arranged as 23 pairs, with one member of each pair inherited from each parent at the time of conception. After conception, these 46 chromosomes duplicate again and again to pass on the same genetic information to each new cell in the developing child.

Offspring of all organisms receive a mixture of genetic information from each parent. This process contributes to the great variation of traits that we see in nature, such as the color of a flower's petals, the markings on a butterfly's wings or a person's hair color, personality or musical talent. Geneticists seek to understand how the information encoded in genes is used and how it is transmitted from one generation to the next. Geneticists also study how tiny variations in genes can disrupt development or cause disease.

Genetic testing has been an important factor in health care since the 1960s, when doctors began urging testing of newborn babies for rare diseases that could be inherited from their parents.

The History of Genetics

Since about 10,000 years ago—the earliest days of plant and animal domestication—humans have understood that characteristic traits of parents could be transmitted to their offspring. For centuries, however, people were unable to reconcile many confusing observations about the mechanisms of inheritance. The scientific study of genetics did not begin until the late 19th century.

The first person to make sense of this complex subject was Austrian monk Gregor Mendel, who conducted a series of experiments on pea plants beginning in the 1850s. Mendel observed the results of crossbreeding plants with different characteristics, such as height, flower color and seed shape. His conclusions from these experiments led him to develop explanations for how traits are transmitted from generation to generation. Mendel's theories form the foundation of modern genetics.

Genetic testing has been an important factor in health care since the 1960s, when doctors began urging testing of newborn babies for rare diseases that could be inherited from their parents. Scientists discovered that phenylketonuria (PKU), a rare disease that causes mental retardation, could be prevented with a special diet if the disease is detected early. Tests for PKU and other rare but treatable diseases now are performed routinely after the birth of a baby.

Scientists predict that in a few years, the sequencing of a patient's entire genome will be an affordable, standardized tool for health care professionals.

In the 1970s, researchers developed genetic tests that could be performed before the birth of a baby. Scientists found that if a mother and father both carry the gene for a certain illness, their child had a high possibility of being born with that disease. Soon, couples thinking of having children could be tested for genes that put their children at risk for developing diseases such as sickle cell anemia (a serious blood disorder) and Tay-Sachs disease (a fatal lipid [fat] storage disorder). By the 1980s, prenatal genetic tests to determine the risk of genetic disease were done frequently; now these tests are a routine part of health care in most states.

In the 1990s, researchers were able to identify genes that revealed a person's chance of developing breast cancer and colon cancer. People with certain forms of a gene called BRCA-1, for example, are more likely to develop breast cancer. In this case, genetic testing helps to determine a person's genetic predisposition to certain diseases—to indicate whether certain gene variations mean a person is more likely to develop a disease. Likelihood, of course, does not equal destiny; it only means the person has a greater possibility of developing the disease than people with other versions of the gene. By the early 2000s, computers and other technology had advanced to the point where large collections of a person's genes could be looked at in a method called genetic profiling.

Genetic tests can be performed to confirm a suspected diagnosis, to predict the possibility of future illness, to detect the presence of a carrier state in unaffected individuals whose children may be at risk and to predict response to therapy. Tests also are performed to screen for genetic defects in newborn babies, fetuses and embryos used in in vitro fertilization. As the number of available tests continues to rise (tests, for example, that predict drug responsiveness for cancer, heart disease and asthma were under way as of April 2006), their use in the health care setting surely will rise as well. Scientists predict that in a few years, the sequencing of a patient's entire genome will be an affordable, standardized tool for health care professionals.

The Science of Genetic Testing

Genetic testing uses gene tests such as DNA testing as well as biochemical tests or protein testing to indicate possible inherited disorders or disease in individuals. Geneticists group genetic disorders into three categories.

Single-Gene Disorders

These are caused by a mistake in a single gene. The mutation may be present on one or both chromosomes of a pair. Sickle cell disease, cystic fibrosis and Tay-Sachs disease are examples of single-gene disorders.

Chromosome Disorders

These are caused by an excess or deficiency of genes. For example, Down syndrome is caused by an extra copy of a chromosome, but no individual gene on the chromosome is abnormal.

Multifactorial Inheritance Disorders

These are caused by a combination of small variations in genes, often in concert with environmental factors. Heart disease, most cancers and Alzheimer's disease are examples of these disorders.

In one type of genetic test, DNA is taken from a person's blood, body fluids or tissues and examined for an abnormality that flags a disease or disorder. The abnormality can be relatively large—a piecc of a chromosome or an entire chromosome, missing or added. Sometimes the change is very small—one extra, missing or altered chemical base within the DNA strand. Genes can be amplified (too many copies), overexpressed (too active), inactivated or lost altogether. Sometimes, pieces of chromosomes become switched, transposed or discovered in an incorrect location.

Genetic testing uses a variety of techniques to examine a person's DNA. Some tests involve using probes, or short strings of DNA, with base sequences complementary to those of the mutated gene. These probes will seek their complements within an individual's genome. If the mutated sequence is present in the patient's genome, the probe will find it and bind to it, flagging the mutation.

Another type of genetic test involves comparing the sequence of DNA bases in a patient's gene to a normal version of the gene.

Biochemical genetic tests look for the presence or absence of key proteins which signal abnormal or malfunctioning genes.

Many diffcrent types of body fluids and tissues can be used in genetic testing. For DNA screening, only a tiny bit of blood, skin, bone or other tissue is needed. Even the small amount of tissue at the bottom end of a human hair usually is enough, and that is why DNA testing often is used successfully by forensic scientists to identify human remains or as part of criminal investigations.

Prenatal Testing

For genetic testing performed in children before their birth, amniocentesis or chorionic villus sampling typically are used. Amniocentesis is a test performed on a pregnant woman, usually between her 16th and 18th week of pregnancy, in which a doctor removes a small amount of amniotic fluid from around the developing fetus. This fluid can be tested to check for genetic problems and to determine the sex of the child. Chorionic villus sampling (CVS) is a test performed on a pregnant woman, usually between the 10th and 12th weeks of pregnancy. In CVS, a doctor removes a small piece of the placenta to check for genetic problems. Both chorionic villus sampling and amniocentesis carry a slight risk of inducing a miscarriage.

Now that a draft of the human genome map is complete, research is focusing on the function of each individual human gene and the role that faulty genes play in disease. Scientists predict this will lead to improved diagnosis of diseases and to a new approach to disease therapy.

Genetic testing can be predictive, discovering whether an individual has an inherited disposition to a certain disease before symptoms appear. Genetic tests also can confirm a diagnosis if symptoms are present.

In most circumstances people undergoing genetic testing meet with a genetic counselor to explore the implications of their test results.

What's more, genetic tests can determine whether a person is a carrier for a disease. Carriers won't get the disease, but they can pass the faulty gene on to their children. Prenatal testing can help expectant parents know whether their unborn child will have a genetic disease or disorder. Newborn screening tests infants for abnormal or missing gene products.

Individuals in families at high risk for a disease live with troubling uncertainties about their own future as well as their children's future. A negative test—especially one that is strongly predictive—can provide an enormous sense of relief to the individuals tested and to their families.

A positive test also can produce benefits. In the best circumstances, a positive test enables a person to take steps to reduce risk. These steps could include regular screening for the disease or lifestyle changes such as a change in diet or exercise. A positive test can relieve uncertainty and enable people to make informed decisions about their future.

In most circumstances people undergoing genetic testing meet with a genetic counselor to explore the implications of their test results. Genetic counselors are health care professionals with specialized graduate degrees and experience in medical genetics and counseling. They work as members of health care teams, providing information and support to individuals or families who have genetic disorders or might be at risk for inherited conditions.

Genetic counselors help assess the risk of a genetic disorder by researching a family's history and evaluating medical records; weigh the medical, social and ethical decisions surrounding genetic testing; provide support and information to help a person make a decision about testing; interpret the results of genetic tests and medical data; provide counseling or refer individuals and families to support services; serve as patient advocates; explain possible treatments or preventive measures; and discuss reproductive options.

Ethical and Social Considerations

Genetic testing has improved many lives dramatically. For supporters, the possibilities are endless. Critics, however, feel uncertainties surrounding test interpretation, quality of life issues, lack of available medical options, the tests' potential for provoking anxiety and the risks of discrimination and social stigmatization could outweigh the benefits of genetic testing. Both supporters and opponents of genetic testing have to consider both the potential moral aspects of genetic testing and the impact of genetic testing on our society as a whole.

Most people would agree that genetic testing has the ability to affect human lives profoundly. Some genetic tests are used to clarify a diagnosis and to direct a physician toward appropriate treatments; other tests allow families to decide whether to have children with devastating diseases. Still, some tests help identify people at high risk for conditions that might be preventable. Aggressive monitoring for and removal of colon growths in those inheriting a gene for familial adenomatous polyposis, for example, has saved many lives. On the horizon is a gene test that will provide doctors with a simple diagnostic test for a common iron-storage disease, transforming it from a usually fatal condition to a treatable one.

Some people fear that testing for the presence of genes eventually could lead to discrimination by employers or insurance companies.

While advances in genetic testing have created a revolution in the way doctors diagnose and treat certain illnesses, many believe there are limits that need to be recognized. First, although genetic tests can identify a particular problem gene, these tests cannot always predict how severely that gene will affect the person who carries it. Second, simply having problem genes is only half the story, because many illnesses develop from a deadly mix of high-risk genes and unhealthy lifestyle (a smoker with a family history of heart disease, for example). However, knowledge of high-risk genes actually might be an advantage, because it gives an individual the chance to modify his or her lifestyle to avoid becoming sick. Third, some people fear that testing for the presence of specific genes eventually could lead to discrimination by employers or insurance companies, to privacy and disclosure disputes and even to the possibility that parents one day might be able to preselect certain genetic characteristics for their children.

Testing for Adult-Onset Disorders

Commercialized genetic tests for adult-onset disorders such as Alzheimer's disease and some cancers are the subject of passionate debate over genetic testing. These tests are targeted to healthy (presymptomatic) people who are identified as being at high risk because of a strong family medical history for the disorder. The tests give only a probability for developing the disorder. One of the most serious limitations of these susceptibility tests is the difficulty in interpreting a positive result, because some people who carry a disease-associated mutation never develop the disease.

Every day, researchers are finding new evidence that people who have specific genes are at a greater risk for illnesses such as cancer, diabetes, heart disease, Alzheimer's disease, psychiatric disorders and many other medical problems. Many researchers believe that the major genetic factors involved in susceptibility to these common diseases will be uncovered over the next decade and that the door to wider availability of genetic testing will open to virtually everyone. This could usher in a new era of individualized preventive medicine, resulting in considerable health benefits. It also could usher in an era of widespread discrimination.

It is important to remember that most of these tests will not definitely answer "yes" or "no," but will *predict* relative risk. For this paradigm to succeed, it will be essential to use predictive genetic information to improve the quality of people's lives—and never for the purpose of discrimination.

Regulation and Legislation

The Advisory Committee on Genetics, Health and Society, staffed by the National Institutes of Health's Office of Biotechnology Activities, provides policy advice to the Department of Health and Human Services (DHHS) on the broad array of complex medical, ethical, legal and social issues raised by genetic testing.

Like other diagnostic laboratory tests, genetic tests are subject to some federal regulatory oversight when they are performed for the purpose of detecting diseases or conditions, or predisposition to such diseases or conditions. Currently, genetic tests are subject to regulation through three statutory and regulatory mechanisms: the Clinical Laboratory Improvement Amendments (CLIA) of 1988, the Federal Food, Drug, and Cosmetic Act as amended in December 2004 and applicable regulations for the protection of human subjects, during the investigational phases of test development.

Four agencies within DHHS have roles in the oversight of genetic test development and use: the Centers for Medicare and Medicaid Services, the Food and Drug Administration, the Centers for Disease Control and Prevention and the Office for Human Research Protections. Other agencies within the department support research activities and demonstration projects that generate knowledge and experience concerning genetic testing.

State health agencies, particularly state public health laboratories, have an oversight role in genetic testing, including the licensure of personnel and facilities that perform genetic tests. State public health laboratories and state-operated licensure programs that have been deemed equivalent to the federal CLIA program are responsible for quality assurance activities. States may impose requirements more stringent than the requirements of CLIA but must, at a minimum, meet federal requirements. States also administer newborn screening programs and provide other genetic services through maternal and child health programs.

Other organizations, such as the American Academy of Pediatrics, the American College of Obstetrics and Gynecology, the American Society of Human Genetics and the National Society of Genetic Counselors, also are involved in the development of guidelines and recommendations regarding the appropriate use of genetic tests. Patient advocacy groups, as well as individuals and families with genetic conditions, also play an important role in setting standards and in developing guidelines through advocacy and monitoring of health care practices.

12

Medical Testing in Developing Countries Is Conducted Ethically

Todd D. Clark

Todd D. Clark is president of VOI Consulting, a life sciences advisory and publishing company. He prepared this white paper for the Association of Clinical Research Organizations (ACRO), which represents the world's foremost clinical research organizations and is a leading voice for safe and ethical clinical trials worldwide.

Although the practice of conducting medical testing in developing countries has received great scrutiny in recent years, the fact is that most trials are done safely and ethically. Clinical trials in emerging countries are conducted using the same standards used in the developed world because the quality of research results depends on it. Such studies also play an important role in improving the economies and health delivery systems in the host countries by way of introducing not just dollars but medical equipment and training. A growing awareness of the need for better regulation and accountability has increased protections for study participants in recent years, and companies that engage in medical testing realize that such practices—whether required by law or not—are good for business.

Todd D. Clark, *The Case for Globalization: Ethical and Business Considerations in Clinical Research*. Washington, DC: Association of Clinical Research Organizations (ACRO), July 2009. Reproduced by permission of ACRO.

As clinical trials have become increasingly globalized over the past ten to fifteen years, the possibility of conducting studies that offer adequate subject protection and yield reliable results in emerging countries has understandably attracted considerable attention. In this analysis, we examine the facts regarding the current state of clinical research and the role that biopharmaceutical companies and their clinical research organization (CRO) partners play in ensuring that the dual goals of trial safety and quality are met.

Although concerns have been raised about the globalization of biomedical research, the reality is that emerging countries play a vital role in the advancement of medical science. Clinical trials in these countries, particularly those with industry sponsorship, are conducted at the high standards necessary to obtain regulatory approval in major markets. In addition, the investments made by trial sponsors, which are frequently implemented by CROs, are a major contributor to improving the health systems and economies of the developing world.

Among the key findings of this report:

- Increased demand for clinical trial subjects combined with lower participation rates in developed countries has the potential to dramatically slow the progress of medical science. Indeed, VOI Consulting estimates that it would require approximately 5.8 years to fully enroll all currently open Phase III cancer trials if only U.S. locations were used as compared to 1.9 years using both U.S. and global trial sites.

- While trials in emerging countries have received an enormous amount of attention in recent years, the vast majority of clinical research continues to be conducted in countries with well-established infrastructures. A few statistics point out just how big a role the U.S., Western Europe and other developed regions continue to play:

- Member companies of the Pharmaceutical Research and Manufacturers of America (PhRMA) spent approximately 96% of clinical phase dollars in developed countries during 2007.

- In its September 2008 report on CROs, Frost & Sullivan estimates that North America has a 49% share of global R&D [research and development] spending while Western Europe had a 37% share. The share for Asia Pacific, a region that includes established markets such as Japan and Australia as well as emerging centers such as India and China, is approximately 13.5%, and the rest of the world has only 0.5%.

- Seventy-six percent of all Phase I studies take place in just three countries, the U.S., Canada and the Netherlands.

- Analysis of data from ClinicalTrials.gov shows that 51.8% of all newly registered industry-sponsored trials in 2008 had at least some U.S. activity; the exact same share as in 2006. This compares with India's 2.7% participation rate, China's 1.8%, Russia's 3.3% and Mexico's 2.4%.

Clinical research plays an important role in improving the health systems and economies of emerging countries.

Standards Are the Same

Trials in emerging countries are subject to the same standards that prevail in the developed world. This is especially true of industry-sponsored trials as these are ultimately aimed at gaining regulatory approval for new products. To engage in unethical or poor quality research is to run the risk that the product will be rejected, leaving the sponsor no way to recoup their R&D investments. The power of the market to correct improper practices is shown by a 2009 incident in which a U.S.-based commercial Institutional Review Board was forced to close due to client losses just one week after receiving an FDA warning letter.

Regulatory and cultural norms regarding clinical research in emerging countries are often more, rather than less, strict than in developed regions. Examples of this include the difficulty of conducting early phase studies in India and placebo-based studies in Latin America. Patients in these countries may also seek greater input from friends and family before deciding to enroll in a trial.

Clinical research plays an important role in improving the health systems and economies of emerging countries. In Poland, for example, 30% of hospital cancer therapy is funded by clinical trial sponsors.

The term "emerging market" disguises a wide range of experience levels. After 15 years of experience with clinical trials, capabilities of the larger Central European countries are considered to be very nearly on a par with those in Western Europe. Other countries, such as South Korea and Taiwan, have advanced medical infrastructures and should be considered "emerging" only in the sense that their trial activity is growing rapidly.

Ethical research norms are global in nature and do not vary from place to place.

Working with CROs offers a number of advantages for sponsors involved in emerging country trials. In addition to the benefits of reduced costs and faster time to market, CROs provide standardization of operating procedures (SOPs) and, at the same time, are more likely to have a deeper understanding of local language, culture and norms, qualities which lead to better relations with investigators and improved trial execution.

The presence of CROs benefits host countries as well. They provide advanced equipment and trained personnel, offer high paying jobs in areas where employment opportunities are scarce and have been instrumental in harmonizing research norms in emerging countries with developed world standards. . . .

Although legitimate concerns have been raised in the past about clinical trials in emerging countries, the ability to conduct high quality studies in these locations has been enormously improved over the previous ten to fifteen years. The research infrastructures in Central and Eastern European as well as in several East Asian countries, which were among the first emerging areas to participate in trials, are now comparable to those in well-established regions. Countries that began hosting studies more recently are also making rapid progress to ensure that they are able to attract clinical trials and the benefits that trials provide. Biopharmaceutical firms and their CRO partners have played and continue to play a leading role in advancing research capabilities throughout the world.

Restricting the ability of emerging countries to participate in clinical research would add still more expenses and further delay the ability of patients to access new therapies.

Ethical Research Norms Are Global

As we have seen, ethical research norms are global in nature and do not vary from place to place. Further, commercial sponsors have very strong incentives to ensure that their investments in clinical research will be accepted by regulatory agencies in the developed countries where they earn the vast majority of their revenues. Indeed, companies that work exclusively in the clinical research field can easily be forced out of business by market forces that demand strict compliance with these ethical rules.

In light of growing activity in emerging countries, major regulatory agencies have recognized the need for greater oversight of international trials and are responding with a substantial commitment of resources to ensure that all research meets the highest ethical and quality standards. There are now more inspections than in the past and these are taking place at an earlier stage than has traditionally been the case. This is a welcome move that provides yet another level of confidence that studies will yield reliable results while providing a safe environment for patients.

The advance of medical science is leading to more clinical trials and these trials are increasingly complex, time-consuming and expensive. Restricting the ability of emerging countries to participate in clinical research would add still more expenses and further delay the ability of patients to access new therapies. It would also deny an important source of investment, employment, health care and knowledge transfer to areas that are desperately in need of all these things. Rather than placing further barriers to drug development, efforts should be focused on enhancing the progress that has already been made while continuing to train and monitor researchers throughout the world to ensure their compliance with the highest standards. Fortunately, much of this is already being done as part of the normal business practices of biopharmaceutical companies and CROs, all of whom have a major stake in a strong and improving clinical research environment.

13

Ethicists Disagree About Medical Testing Without Consent During Crises

Rob Stein

Rob Stein is a staff writer for the Washington Post.

Studies to test new potentially lifesaving treatments for trauma and cardiac arrest are being conducted without patient consent because the experimental treatments are administered only in life-threatening situations in which the participants are unconscious. Medical professionals disagree about whether the studies violate ethical principles or whether they are ethically justified. Critics argue that emergency responders should not take unnecessary chances by administering unproven treatments when they are trying to save someone's life and that it is unethical because the participants themselves have not consented to accepting such a risk. Proponents of the testing argue that there is no real ethical problem because most people die with the currently available treatments and the experimental treatments may work better.

The federal government is undertaking the most ambitious set of studies ever mounted under a controversial arrangement that allows researchers to conduct some kinds of medical experiments without first getting patients' permission.

The $50 million, five-year project, which will involve more than 20,000 patients in 11 sites in the United States and Canada, is designed to improve treatment after car accidents, shootings, cardiac arrest and other emergencies.v

Rob Stein, "Critical Care Without Consent—Ethicists Disagree On Experimenting During Crises," *Washington Post*, May 27, 2007. Reproduced by permission.

The three studies, organizers say, offer an unprecedented opportunity to find better ways to resuscitate people whose hearts suddenly stop, to stabilize patients who go into shock and to minimize damage from head injuries. Because such patients are usually unconscious at a time when every minute counts, it is often impossible to get consent from them or their families, the organizers say.

The project has been endorsed by many trauma experts and some bioethicists. Others question it. The harshest critics say the research violates fundamental ethical principles.

The organizers said the studies are going forward only after an exhaustive scientific and ethical review by the National Institutes of Health, which authorized the funding in 2004, and the Food and Drug Administration [FDA], which approved the first phase about a year ago [in May 2006] and the second phase six months ago [in December 2006].

The studies are being conducted by the Resuscitation Outcomes Consortium, a network of medical centers that do research in Seattle, Portland, San Diego, Dallas, Birmingham, Pittsburgh, Milwaukee, Toronto and Ottawa, and in Iowa and British Columbia.

Testing Life-Saving Interventions

The first experiments, involving nearly 6,000 patients, involve patients who are in shock or have suffered head injuries from a car crash, a fall or some other trauma.

About 40,000 such patients show up at hospitals each year, and the standard practice is to give them saline infusions to stabilize their blood pressure. For the study, emergency medical workers are randomly infusing some patients with "hypertonic" solutions containing much higher levels of sodium, with or without a drug called dextran. Animal research and small human studies have indicated that hypertonic solutions could save more lives and minimize brain damage.

The next experiment, which will involve about 15,000 patients, is designed to determine how best to revive patients whose hearts suddenly stop beating. About 180,000 Americans suffer these sudden cardiac arrests each year.

We will never know the best way to treat people unless we do this research. And the only way we can do this research, since the person is unconscious, is without consent.

Emergency medical workers often shock these patients immediately to try to get their hearts started again. But some do a few minutes of cardiopulmonary resuscitation [CPR] first. Researchers want to determine which tactic works better by randomly trying one or the other—both with and without a special valve attached to devices used to push air into the lungs during CPR. That study is expected to start next month [June 2007].

"We will never know the best way to treat people unless we do this research. And the only way we can do this research, since the person is unconscious, is without consent," said Myron L. Weisfeldt of the Johns Hopkins University School of Medicine, who is overseeing the project. "Even if there are family members present, they know their loved one is dying. The ambulance is there. The sirens are going off. You can't possibly imagine gaining a meaningful informed consent from someone under those circumstances."

Before starting the research at each site, researchers complete a "community consultation" process. Local organizers try to notify the public about the study and gauge the reaction through public meetings, telephone surveys, Internet postings and advertisements, and through reports in local news media. Anyone who objects can get a special bracelet to alert medical workers that they refuse to participate.

The project proceeds only after also being vetted by a set of local independent reviewers known as an institutional review board. Another group of independent advisers known as a data safety monitoring board will periodically review the study for any signs of problems.

Concept Sparks Debate

Despite such oversight, some previous similar projects have sparked intense debate. Most recently, a study testing a blood substitute called PolyHeme was criticized for putting patients at risk without consent.

In fact, concerns raised by the PolyHeme study and others prompted the FDA to launch a review of the entire program that permits experiments to be done without consent in emergency situations.

"The ethics and policy concern is how you balance the streamlining of research to get the best information to treat patients against the moral imperative to get consent," said Nancy M.P. King, a bioethicist at Wake Forest University School of Medicine. "The emergency consent exception is supposed to carve out a very narrow window. What's been happening is that narrow window seems to be expanding."

This just seems like lazy investigators not wanting to try to get informed consent in situations where it is difficult to get it, so they say it is impossible.

Some bioethicists say the new research is more ethical than some of the earlier studies in several ways, including that patients are not being denied highly effective therapies. Most patients who receive the current treatments do not survive.

"I understand why there might be concerns, but I think ethically this is permissible," said Arthur R. Derse, a bioethicist at the Medical College of Wisconsin, which refused to participate in the PolyHeme study. "The treatments we currently have are unsatisfactory."

But others say that the studies could be done by finding patients or family members who are in a position to provide consent, even though that might make such studies more difficult.

"This just seems like lazy investigators not wanting to try to get informed consent in situations where it is difficult to get it, so they say it is impossible," said George J. Annas, a Boston University bioethicist. "I don't think we should use people like this."

Annas was particularly disturbed that children as young as 15 might be included in the research.

Taking Chances

"Suppose a 15-year-old child is in the back of a car that is in a terrible accident," Annas said. "The EMTs [emergency medical technicians] arrive and say: 'We are doing an experiment with two techniques. We think they are about equal. Is it okay if we flip a coin to see how we treat your son? Or would you rather we just give him the treatment we think is best?' Unless you think all parents would have the EMTs flip a coin, consent here is necessary."

Others are concerned patients may be getting experimental therapies that could turn out to be inferior to standard treatments.

"The most promising experimental medical interventions have often been shown to be less effective than standard treatment," said Kenneth Kipnis, a University of Hawaii bioethicist.

The "community consultation" process has also come under fire.

"Community consultation is intended to be a collaboration with the community of potential subjects, not just letting them know what the plan is," said King, the Wake Forest bioethicist.

But Weisfeldt at Johns Hopkins said the critics would be unhappy under any circumstances.

"Some people object to the whole concept of doing any study whatsoever without permission," Weisfeldt said. "We try to explain all the layers of approval we've gone through and that this is the only way we can do the kind of research that could save many more lives in the future."

Organizations to Contact

The editors have compiled the following list of organizations concerned with the issues debated in this book. The descriptions are derived from materials provided by the organizations. All have publications or information available for interested readers. The list was compiled on the date of publication of the present volume; names, addresses, phone and fax numbers, and e-mail and Internet addresses may change. Be aware that many organizations take several weeks or longer to respond to inquiries, so allow as much time as possible.

Centers for Disease Control and Prevention (CDC)
1600 Clifton Rd., Atlanta, GA   30333
(800) 232-4636
e-mail: tuskegeeinquiries@cdc.gov
website: www.cdc.gov/tuskegee

The Centers for Disease Control and Prevention maintains a website called "US Public Health Service Syphilis Study at Tuskegee," which is dedicated to providing information about the infamous 1932 Tuskegee experiment. The site includes a comprehensive overview of the study, information about syphilis, frequently asked questions, a detailed timeline, a section about research implications, and the formal governmental apology to the men and their families from President Bill Clinton in 1997. The CDC site also includes a link to the National Archives, which hosts patient files and historic photographs from the Tuskegee study.

CenterWatch
10 Winthrop Sq., 5th Floor, Boston, MA   02110
(617) 948-5100
e-mail: press@centerwatch.com
website: www.centerwatch.com

CenterWatch, the leading publisher of information on clinical research for patients and their advocates, operates a website called The Healthlinks Clinical Trials Resource Center. The site offers extensive information about what to expect when participating in clinical research, an international listing of clinical trials that are actively recruiting patients in the United States and internationally, a comprehensive listing of drugs that recently have been approved by the Food and Drug Administration, a directory of detailed profiles of more than nine hundred clinical research centers, and news articles and reports on recent advances in clinical research. The "Patient Bookstore" page of the site contains a variety of reports, brochures, and publications that patients and their advocates can use to learn about the clinical trials industry and how to identify and volunteer for clinical trials.

Foundation for Biomedical Research (FBR)

818 Connecticut Ave. NW, Suite 900, Washington, DC 20006
(202) 457-0654 • fax: (202) 457-0659
e-mail: info@fbresearch.org
website: www.fbresearch.org

Established in 1981, the Foundation for Biomedical Research is dedicated to improving human and veterinary health by promoting public understanding and support for humane and responsible animal research. The FBR website offers a special education page for students to explore these issues. Brochures such as *Animal Rights Activism, AIDS and Animal Research*, and *The Importance of Being a Mouse* are available from the site, which also maintains a page of links for further research on the topic of animal testing. The organization publishes a monthly magazine titled *Research Saves*.

National Human Genome Research Institute

National Institutes of Health Building 31, Room 4B09
31 Center Dr., MSC 2152, 9000 Rockville Pike
Bethesda, MD 20892-2152
(301) 402-0911 • fax: (301) 402-2218
website: www.genome.gov

The National Human Genome Research Institute began as the National Center for Human Genome Research (NCHGR), which was established in 1989 to carry out the role of the National Institutes of Health (NIH) in the International Human Genome Project (HGP). The HGP began in 1990 to map the human genome. In 1997 the Department of Health and Human Services renamed NCHGR the National Human Genome Research Institute, officially elevating it to the status of a research institute—one of twenty-seven institutes and centers that make up the NIH. The National Human Genome Research Institute website provides access to hundreds of articles related to genetic testing. It features an extensive collection of material specifically regarding ethics, including the publications "Policy and Ethics Issues," "The Ethics of Synthetic Biology and Emerging Technologies," and "What Is the Role of Ethics and Genetic Counseling?"

National Institutes of Health (NIH)

9000 Rockville Pike, Bethesda, MD   20892
(301) 496-4000
e-mail: nihinfo@od.nih.gov
website: www.nih.gov

Founded in 1887, the National Institutes of Health is one of the world's foremost medical research centers as well as the federal focal point for medical research in the United States. The NIH, which comprises twenty-seven separate institutes and centers, is one of eight health agencies of the Public Health Service, which in turn is part of the cabinet-level US Department of Health and Human Services. The NIH website describes federal policies and brings indepth information about medical testing to the scientific community and general public. NIH fact sheets on medical experimentation, genetic testing, clinical trials, human subjects protection, and research ethics are available for download from the site, as is the report "Ensuring Responsible Research."

People for the Ethical Treatment of Animals (PETA)

501 Front St., Norfolk, VA   23510
(757) 622-7382 • fax: (757) 622-0457
website: www.peta.org

People for the Ethical Treatment of Animals is the largest animal rights organization in the world, with more than two million members and supporters. It strongly opposes medical testing on animals and it devotes a large part of its website to the issue. The "Animals Used for Experimentation" section of PETA's website includes extensive information about animal research, including graphic photos. The site also includes dozens of articles and links pertaining to the use of animals in research, as well as links to other organizations and resources related to the topic. Position papers, such as "Tell It Like It Is: Animal Research Is Murder," can be downloaded from the site. The regularly updated *PETA Files* blog includes such items as "Top Five Reasons to Stop Animal Testing," and "Who's to Blame for Half of All Animal Testing?"

Pharmaceutical Research and Manufacturers of America (PhRMA)

950 F St. NW, Suite 300, Washington, DC 20004
(202) 835-3400 • fax: (202) 835-3414
website: www.phrma.org

The Pharmaceutical Research and Manufacturers of America represents US drug research and biotechnology companies. It advocates public policies that encourage discovery of important medicines, and its medical officers testify before Congress on issues such as the safety of clinical trials for new drugs, foreign clinical trials, and testing pharmaceutical products on human subjects. PhRMA's website offers dozens of articles related to those topics, including "PhRMA Guiding Principles: Statement on Foreign Clinical Trials," and "Clinical Trials—So Necessary, Now More Complex than Ever."

The Presidential Commission for the Study of Bioethical Issues

1425 New York Ave. NW, Suite C-100, Washington, DC 20005
(202) 233-3960 • fax: (202) 233-3990
e-mail: info@bioethics.gov
website: www.bioethics.gov

The commission advises the president on bioethical issues that may emerge from advances in biology and medicine and related areas of science and technology. The commission works to identify and promote policies and practices that ensure scientific research, health care delivery, and technological innovation are conducted in an ethically responsible manner. The commission's website hosts an extensive archive of public testimony, white papers, and presentations regarding the ethics of genetic testing, synthetic biology, and human subjects protection. Full transcripts from all of the commission's meetings are also available from the site. A bioethics blog on the site includes posts with such titles as "A New Start Looking at Overseas Clinical Trials," and "Ethics of Genetic Prenatal Tests."

US Department of Health and Human Services, Office for Human Research Protections (OHRP)

1101 Wootton Pkwy., Suite 200, Rockville, MD   20852
(866) 447-4777 • fax: (240) 453-6909
e-mail: ohrp@hhs.gov
website: www.hhs.gov/ohrp

The US Department of Health and Human Services runs the Office for Human Research Protections. The role of OHRP is to protect the rights, welfare, and well-being of subjects involved in research. OHRP provides clarification and guidance, develops educational programs and materials, maintains regulatory oversight, and provides advice on ethical and regulatory issues in biomedical and behavioral research. Its website includes special sections that focus on children in research, conflict of interest, and international issues. A wealth of historical documents can be downloaded from the site, including the Nuremburg Code, the Declaration of Helsinki, and the Belmont Report. A complete list of all of the federal rules and regulations pertaining to human subjects research also is available.

Bibliography

Books

Roberto Abadie   *The Professional Guinea Pig: Big Pharma and the Risky World of Human Subjects.* Durham, NC: Duke University Press, 2010.

George Annas and Michael Grodin   *The Nazi Doctors and the Nuremberg Code: Human Rights in Human Experimentation.* New York: Oxford University Press, 1995.

Baruch Brody   *The Ethics of Biomedical Research: An International Perspective.* New York: Oxford University Press, 1998.

Dena Davis   *Genetic Dilemmas: Reproductive Technology, Parental Choices, and Children's Futures.* 2nd ed. New York: Oxford University Press, 2009.

Andrew Goliszek   *In the Name of Science.* New York: St. Martin's, 2003.

Michael Grodin and Leonard Glantz   *Children as Research Subjects: Science, Ethics, and Law.* New York: Oxford University Press, 1994.

Sydney Halpern   *Lesser Harms: The Morality of Risk in Medical Research.* Chicago: University of Chicago Press, 2006.

Jennifer Hawkins and Ezekiel Emanuel   *Exploitation and Developing Countries: The Ethics of Clinical Research.* Princeton, NJ: Princeton University Press, 2008.

Allen Hornblum *Acres of Skin: Human Experiments at Holmesburg Prison: A Story of Abuse and Exploitation in the Name of Medical Science.* New York: Routledge, 1998.

A.J. Jacobs *The Guinea Pig Diaries: My Life as an Experiment.* New York: Simon & Schuster, 2009.

Susan Reverby *Examining Tuskegee: The Infamous Syphilis Study and Its Legacy.* Chapel Hill: University of North Carolina Press, 2009.

Lainie Friedman Ross *Children in Medical Research: Access Versus Protection.* Oxford, United Kingdom: Oxford University Press, 2008.

Jane Runzheimer and Linda Johnson Larsen *Medical Ethics for Dummies.* Hoboken, NJ: Wiley, 2010.

Sonia Shah *The Body Hunters: Testing New Drugs on the World's Poorest Patients.* New York: New Press, 2007.

Harriet Washington *Medical Apartheid: The Dark History of Medical Experimentation on Black Americans from Colonial Times to the Present.* New York: Doubleday, 2007.

Periodicals and Internet Sources

Donald L. Barlett and James B. Steele "Deadly Medicine," *Vanity Fair,* January 2011.

BBC News   "Hidden History of US Germ
                     Testing," February 13, 2006.

BBC News   "Nigerians Angered by Drug Trial
                     Delay," July 30, 2001.

Ethan Blue   "The Strange Career of Leo Stanley:
                     Remaking Manhood and Medicine at
                     San Quentin State Penitentiary,
                     1913–1951," *Pacific Historical Review*,
                     May 2009.

Lauren Hammer   "The Best Pharmaceuticals for
Breslow   Children Act of 2002: The Rise of
                     the Voluntary Incentive Structure and
                     Congressional Refusal to Require
                     Pediatric Testing," *Harvard Journal of
                     Legislation*, Winter 2003.

Gregory Dober   "Cheaper than Chimpanzees:
                     Expanding the Use of Prisoners in
                     Medical Experiments," *Prison Legal
                     News*, March 2008.

Carl Elliott   "The Deadly Corruption of Clinical
                     Trials," *Mother Jones*,
                     September–October 2010.

Carl Elliott   "Guinea-Pigging," *New Yorker*,
                     January 7, 2008.

Amanda Gardner   "Many Clinical Trials Moving
                     Overseas—Study Says Trend Raises
                     Ethical, Medical Issues," *US News and
                     World Report*, February 18, 2009.

Seth Glickman et al. — "Ethical and Scientific Implications of the Globalization of Clinical Research," *New England Journal of Medicine*, February 19, 2009.

Christine Grady — "Do IRBs Protect Human Research Participants?" *Journal of the American Medical Association*, September 8, 2010.

Amy Harmon — "Insurance Fears Lead Many to Shun DNA Tests," *New York Times*, February 24, 2008.

Kaiser Family Foundation — "President Bush Signs Genetic Nondiscrimination Legislation into Law," *Kaiser Daily Health Policy Report*, May 22, 2008.

Brandon Keim — "Genetic Discrimination by Insurers, Employers Becomes a Crime," *Wired*, May 21, 2008.

Donald McNeill Jr. — "U.S. Apologizes for Syphilis Tests in Guatemala," *New York Times*, October 1, 2010.

Laura Parker — "'Bad Blood' Still Flows in Tuskegee Study," *USA Today*, January 20, 2009.

Sheldon Richman — "Did the CIA Conduct Medical Experiments on Detainees?" *Counterpunch*, June 23, 2010.

Amaya Rivera — "Medical Apartheid," *Mother Jones*, January 5, 2007.

Ian Urbina   "Panel Suggests Using Inmates in
                          Drug Trials," *New York Times*, August
                          13, 2006.

Shawna Williams   "Direct-to-Consumer Genetic
and Gail Javitt   Testing: Empowering or Endangering
                          the Public?," Genetics and Public
                          Policy Center, July 25, 2006.
                          www.dnapolicy.org.

Index

A

Adenomatous polyposis, 100

Advance directives, 73–74

Advisory Committee on Genetics, Health and Society, 101–102

African Americans, 9, 13, 72

Age of informed consent, 67–68

AIDS, 19, 52, 78, 87

Alzheimer's disease, 73–74, 87, 89, 97, 101

American Academy of Pediatrics, 67

Amniocentesis, 98

Animal domestication and breeding, 94

Animal rights organizations, 76, 91

Animal testing, 76–82, 83–91
  alternatives to, 81–82, 85–86
  attitudes about, 77, 90–91
  as cruelty to animals, 76–77
  funding and accountability, 79–80
  humane treatment of animals, 88–89
  limitations of, 41
  necessity of, 84–85
  oversight and regulation, 80–81, 87–88
  reduction, replacement and refinement, 85–86
  species statistics, 86–87
  stem cell research and, 89–90
  unreliability and manipulation of results, 77–79

Animal Welfare Act (AWA), 80, 87–88

Annas, George J., 114

Anthony, Edward "Yusef," 18

Antipsychotic drugs, 33–34, 35–36

AstraZeneca, 36

Attitudes about medical research, 12, 14, 17–18, 72, 73

Authorship of medical journal articles, 31

AZT (AIDS drug), 19

B

Beckman, Mary, 39

Belmont Report, 9, 120

Benz, Edward, Jr., 41, 42, 43, 44

Bianco, Richard, 37

Biotechnology companies. See Pharmaceutical industry; Pharmaceutical Research and Manufacturers of America (PhRMA)

Blood drawing from children, 60–61

The Body Hunters (Shah), 8

Boston University, 114

C

CAFE (comparison of atypicals in first-episode schizophrenia) study, 35–36

Cancer
  animal testing, 78, 79
  clinical trial subject recruitment, 105

genetic testing, 95–96, 101
intentional infection of humans, 7, 12, 17–18
IRBs and human subjects protections, 41–42
Caplan, Arthur, 13, 19, 21
Cardiac arrest, 110–111, 112
Cardiopulmonary resuscitation (CPR), 112
Cardozo Clinic, 71–72, 75
Cats, 86–87
Centers for Disease Control and Prevention (CDC), 102, 116
Centers for Medicare and Medicaid Services, 102
Charitable organizations, 79, 82
Children. See Pediatric research
Children's Hospital of Philadelphia, 58
Chorionic villus sampling (CVS), 98
Chromosomes, 93–94, 96
Clinical investigators
    conflicts of interest, 28, 42
    payment to, 26, 29–30, 36
    relationships with study participants, 35
    selection and training of, 25
Clinical Laboratory Improvements Amendments (CLIA) of 1988, 102
Clinical research organizations (CROs), 105, 106, 107–108
Clinical trials
    conflicts of interest, 30–31
    cost considerations, 10, 109
    cultural differences in, 107
    defined, 24
    in developing countries, 10, 110–115

funding of, 24, 31–32, 36, 48, 49, 105, 107
information disclosure, 31–32, 106
monitoring of, 26–27, 28
objectivity safeguards, 28–30
pediatric, 58–63
process overview, 24–27
recruitment of human participants, 43, 105
regulation of, 40–44, 109
See also Institutional Review Boards; International clinical trials/experiments
ClinicalTrials.gov, 106
Clinton, Bill, 9
Cognitively disabled adults, 70–71, 73, 75
Colon polyps, 100
Common Rule protections for prisoners, 53–54
Community consultation process, 112, 114–115
Confidentiality of medical information, 27
Conflicts of interest, 21, 22, 28, 30–31, 33, 35, 42
Consent. See Informed consent
Consent form reading levels, 59
Consortium to Examine Clinical Research Ethics (CECRE), 71
Cornell University Weill Medical College, 42
Council of International Organizations of Medical Sciences (CIOMS), 70
Crises, medical testing during, 110–115
Cruelty to animals. See Animal testing

Cultural differences in clinical trials, 107
Curiosity-satisfying experiments, 12, 13, 15, 69
CVS (chorionic villus sampling), 98
Cystic fibrosis, 96

D

Dana-Farber Cancer Institute, 41
Data and Safety Monitoring Boards (DSMBs), 27, 28
DeBakey, Michael E., 88–89
Declaration of Helsinki, 8, 23
Derse, Arthur R., 113
Developing countries, medical research in, 104–109
    benefits of, 105, 109
    clinical trial standards, 106–107
    as cost control measure, 10
    medical infrastructure growth and, 107–108
    regulation and oversight, 108–109
    See also International clinical trials/experiments
DHHS (Health and Human Services, U.S. Department of), 40, 101–102
Direct benefits to research participants, 59, 60, 67, 68–69, 73
Disclosure of clinical trial information, 31–32, 106
Discrimination, 73–74, 99–101
DNA (deoxyribonucleic acid), 92–94, 97
Dogs, 86–87
Down Syndrome, 96

Dresser, Rebecca, 41–42, 42–43
Drug studies, 33–34
Duke University, 20

E

Economically disadvantaged study participants, 71–72, 75
Emanuel, Ezekiel, 38
Emergency medical treatment experimentation, 110–115
"Ethical Considerations for Research Involving Prisoners" (IOM report), 47–48
Ethics committees. *See* Institutional review boards
Eugenics, 46
Exclusion from research, 71, 72, 73–74

F

Families
    genetic testing and, 99–101
    of participants unable to consent, 33, 58, 59, 61–62, 74, 111–112
FDA. *See* Food and Drug Administration, U.S.
Fetuses, 46, 53, 70, 96, 98
    See also Pregnant women
Fins, Joseph, 42, 44
"First do no harm" oath, 13
Flu, 12, 14, 15
Food, Drug and Cosmetic Act of 2004, 102
Food and Drug Administration, U.S. (FDA), 23, 40–44, 102, 107, 111, 113

Foundation for Biomedical Research, 83, 87, 117
Freedman, Benjamin, 67

G

Genetic counseling, 99
Genetic profiling, 96
Genetic testing, 92–103
    for adult-onset disorders, 101
    defined, 92–93
    ethical and social considerations, 99–101
    history of genetics, 94–96
    prenatal testing, 95, 98
    regulation and legislation, 101–103
    testing techniques, 97
    types of genetic disorders, 96–97
Globalization. *See* Developing countries, medical research in; International clinical trials/experiments
Goldberger, Joseph, 16
Gonorrhea, 15–16
Grady, Christine, 64
Guatemala syphilis experiments, 13, 18, 20–21
Guide for the Care and Use of Laboratory Animals (PHS), 88
Guideline for Good Clinical Practice (ICH), 23

H

Havens, W. Paul, Jr., 14–15
Head injuries, 111

Health and Human Services, U.S. Department of (DHHS), 40, 101–102
Healthy research participants, risks to, 59–60
Hepatitis, 7, 14–15, 18
HHS. *See* Health and Human Services, U.S. Department of
Hippocratic Oath, 13
HIV/AIDS, 19, 52, 78, 87
Holmesburg Prison, 18
Human subjects research
    early objections to, 18–19
    history of, 7–9
    under Nazism, 7, 8, 17, 45–46
    regulation of, 40–44
    See also Clinical trials; Institutional Review Boards; Office of Human Research Protections; Research participants
Hyman, William, 18
Hypertonic solutions, 111

I

Independent review, 28, 113
    See also Institutional Review Boards (IRBs)
Infection, intentional, 7, 13–16, 18, 20
Informed consent
    absence in Guatemalan syphilis study, 20
    community consultation process, 112, 114–115
    under emergency conditions, 110–115
    in Nuremberg Code, 8, 46
    for pediatric research subjects, 59, 60, 61, 65, 67–68

PhRMA statements on, 22, 26, 29
of prisoners, 53
of vulnerable individuals, 64, 65, 72–73
Institute of Medicine (IOM)
Guatemala syphilis probe, 21
medical testing on prisoners report, 47–48, 51–57
purpose of, 51
Institutional Animal Care and Use Committees (IACUCs), 88
Institutional Review Boards (IRBs), 39–44
complaint investigation, 36
composition of, 59, 60
legal obligations, 36–37
origin of, 8
oversight of, 41–44
overview, 25–26
pediatric trials considerations, 58–63, 65
review of payments to participants, 29
risk assessment, 58, 59–60, 65–67, 69
self-policing, 37–38
as trust-based system, 34–35
vulnerable adults and, 70–71, 74–75
See also Clinical trials; Informed consent
International clinical trials/ experiments
cultural differences and, 107
ethical lapses in, 19–20
PhRMA statement on, 27
U.S. regulations and, 12, 43
See also Clinical trials; Developing countries, medical research in

International Conference on Harmonization (ICH), 23
Into the Ashes (movie), 45–46
Investigators, clinical. *See* Clinical investigators
IRBs. *See* Institutional Review Boards

J

Jewish Chronic Disease Hospital, 17–18
Johns Hopkins University School of Medicine, 112
Johnson, Ken, 10

K

Katz, Ralph V., 9
Keane, Moira, 35
Keys, Ancel, 15
King, Nancy, 69, 113, 115
Kipnis, Kenneth, 114
Klausner, Richard, 78

L

Lab animals. *See* Animal testing
Laypersons as IRB members, 59, 60

M

Malaria, 15
Markingson, Dan, 33–34
Medic alert bracelets, 112
Medical College of Wisconsin, 114
Medical journal article authorship, 31

Medical testing and experimentation. *See* Animal testing; Clinical trials; Human subjects research
Mendel, Gregor, 94–95
Mengele, Josef, 46
Meningitis, 19
Mental patients, 7, 14–15, 18, 20
    See also Vulnerable research populations
Minimal risk standard, 48–49, 66–67
Minorities (racial), 8, 70, 72, 75
    See also African Americans
Monitoring of clinical trials, 26–27, 28
Monkeys, 86–87
Morrison, Tonia, 58
Mulcahy, Tim, 37

N

National Cancer Institute (NCI), 42, 78
National Commission for the Protection of Human Subjects of Biomedical and Behavioral Research (NCPHSBBR), 45, 47, 54, 67, 70–71
National Institute of Arthritis and Musculoskeletal and Skin Diseases (NIAMS), 71
National Institutes of Health (NIH), 64, 65, 71, 74–75, 79, 118
Nazi human experimentation, 7, 8, 17, 45–46
Necessity requirement, 72–73
New York State Vocational Institution, 15
Newborn babies, 53, 95, 96, 98, 102

Nigeria, 19
NIH Clinical Center, 71–72, 75
North Carolina Association for Biomedical Research, 92
Nuremberg Code, 7, 17, 45, 46

O

Obama, Barack, 12, 21
Objectivity in research, 28–30
Office of Human Research Protections (OHRP), 9, 42–43, 49–49, 52, 102, 120
Olson, Jeremy, 33
Olson, Stephen, 35, 36, 37, 38
Out of the Ashes (movie), 46

P

Patuxent Institution, 15
Pediatric research, 58–63
    blood drawing issues, 60–61, 62
    family issues, 61–62
    informed consent issues, 59, 67–68
    risk assessment, 58, 59–60, 65–67, 69
    untested treatments and, 65
Pellagra (illness), 16
People for the Ethical Treatment of Animals (PETA), 76, 118–119
Perl, Gisella, 46
Pfizer Inc., 19
Pharmaceutical industry
    FDA regulation of, 42–43
    financial interests in ethical research, 106–107
    financing of clinical trials, 24, 31–32, 36, 48, 49, 105, 107
    growth of, 17

research in developing world, 10, 19, 108–109
research on prisoners, 17, 18
Pharmaceutical Research and Manufacturers of America (PhRMA), 22–32
   clinical research principles, 23–24
   clinical trials in developing countries, 106
   clinical trials process overview, 24–27
   conflicts of interest, 30–31
   disclosure of clinical trial information, 31–32
   objectivity statement, 28–30
   organizational background, 22–23, 119
   research in developing world, 10
Phase I trials, 60, 106
Phenylketonuria (PKU), 95
Plant domestication and breeding, 94–95
PolyHeme (blood substitute), 113–114
Pope, Harrison, 36
Pregnant women, 7–8, 19, 46, 53, 64–65, 70
   See also Fetuses; Prenatal testing; Vulnerable research populations
Prenatal testing, 95, 98
Prentice, Ernest, 36
Presidential Commission for the Study of Bioethical Issues, 12–13, 119–120
Primates, 86–87
Prisoners, 45–50, 51–57
   access to medical care, 50, 52
   defined, 51, 52

history of experimentation on, 7
intentional infection of, 15–18
IOM recommendations for research on, 47–48, 55–57
ongoing experimentation on, 48–49
regulation of experimentation on, 19, 47–48, 53–54
Privacy of medical information, 27
Public Health Service (PHS) Act, U.S., 88
Public opinion. *See* Attitudes about medical research
Public service employees, 15
PUBMED database, 49
Puglisi, Thomas, 48

Q

Quality assurance, 27

R

Racial minorities, 72, 75
Recruitment of research participants, 34
Report and Recommendations: Research Involving Prisoners (NCPHSBBR), 54
Research advance directives, 73–74
Research participants
   direct benefits to, 59, 60, 67, 68–69, 73
   inability to consent, 73–74
   payment to, 29
   prisoners and mental patients as, 14–20
   protections for, 40–44

reading levels and consent forms, 59
recruitment of, 35, 40
risks to healthy, 59–60
uninsured, 71–72
vulnerable groups of adults as, 69–70
See also Animal testing; Pediatric research; Vulnerable research populations
Resuscitation Outcomes Consortium, 111
Retaliation for whistle blowing, 38
Reverby, Susan, 18
Risk assessment
in clinical trials, 23, 32
for genetic disease, 95–96, 99, 100–101
informed consent and, 26, 74
IRBs and, 34–36 44
minimal risk standard, 48, 67
in pediatric research, 58, 59–60, 65–67, 69
prisoners as research subjects and, 53, 55–56
RNA (ribonuclcic acid), 93

S

Safety monitoring, 26–27, 28
Salk, Jonas, 14
San Quentin State Prison (CA), 16–17
Schizophrenic patients, 33–38
Schulz, Charles, 36
Scientific inquiry-based experimentation, 12, 13, 15, 69, 77
Secretary's Advisory Committee on Human Research Protections (SACHRP), 49–50
Service animals, 84

Shah, Sonia, 8, 10
Shock (medical condition), 111
Shock (medical procedure), 112
Sickle cell anemia, 95, 96
Sponsors of clinical trials. *See* Pharmaceutical industry
Stanley, L.L., 16–17
Stark, Laura, 14, 20
Stem cell research, 89–90
Subpart C prisoner protections, 45, 47, 49, 53–54
Suicide, 33, 35
Sylvester, Donna, 58
Syphilis, 7, 9, 13, 18, 20 21

T

Talvi, Silja J.A., 45
Tay-Sachs disease, 95, 96
Testicle transplantation, 7, 16–17
Tosto, Paul, 33
Tuberculosis, 7
Tuskegee syphilis study, 9, 13, 18

U

Uganda, 19
Uninsured study participants, 71–72
United States Department of Agriculture (USDA), 80–81, 86–87
University of Hawaii, 114
University of Hong Kong Clinical Trials Centre, 10
University of Minnesota, 15, 33–34, 36–38
University of Nebraska Medical Center, 36

University of Pennsylvania Center for Bioethics, 13

Upper Cardozo Clinic, 71–72, 75

V

Vaccines, 14, 15, 22, 78, 90

Vivisections, 7, 10, 46

Vulnerable research populations, 64–75

ability to consent, 72–73

cognitively disabled adults, 70–71, 73, 75

defined, 69–70

history of experimentation on, 7–8

inclusion/exclusion from research, 71–74

mental patients, 7, 14–15, 18, 20

pregnant women, 7–8, 19, 46, 64–65, 70

See also Pediatric research; Prisoners

W

Wake Forest University School of Medicine, 113

Wards of the state, 69

Warren G. Magnuson Clinical Center (NIH), 64

Washington University, 41

Weijer, Charles, 67

Weisfeldt, Myron L., 112, 115

Weiss, Mary, 35, 36

Weiss, Rick, 21

Wendler, David, 64

Wesleyan University, 14

Whistleblower protections, 38

Willowbrook State School, 18

Withholding of care, 7, 19, 33

Wright, Paul, 50